Reengineering
the Organization

Also available from ASQC Quality Press

Process Reengineering: The Key to Achieving Breakthrough Success
Lon Roberts

Reengineering the Factory
A. Richard Shores

Quality: The Ball in Your Court, 2nd Edition
Frank C. Collins, Jr.

Breakthrough Quality Improvements for Leaders Who Want Results
Robert F. Wickman and Robert S. Doyle

The ASQC Total Quality Management Series
    TQM: Leadership for the Quality Transformation
    Richard S. Johnson

    TQM: Management Processes for Quality Operations
    Richard S. Johnson

    TQM: The Mechanics of Quality Processes
    Richard S. Johnson and Lawrence E. Kazense

    TQM: Quality Training Practices
    Richard S. Johnson

To request a complimentary catalog of publications, call 800-248-1946.

Reengineering the Organization

A Step-by-Step Approach to Corporate Revitalization

Jeffrey N. Lowenthal

ASQC Quality Press
Milwaukee, Wisconsin

Reengineering the Organization: A Step-by-Step Approach to Corporate Revitalization
Jeffrey N. Lowenthal

Library of Congress Cataloging-in-Publication Data

Lowenthal, Jeffrey N.
    Reengineering the organization: a step-by-step approach to
corporate revitalization / Jeffrey N. Lowenthal.
        p.   cm.
    Includes bibliographical references and index.
    ISBN 0-87389-258-5
    1. Organizational change—Management.   I. Title
HD58.8.L69   1994
658.4' 063—dc20   93-4774
                                                            CIP

10 9 8 7 6 5 4 3 2

ISBN 0-87389-258-5

Acquisitions Editor: Susan Westergard
Project Editor: Kelley Cardinal
Production Editor: Annette Wall
Marketing Administrator: Mark Olson
Set in Galliard and Optima by Montgomery Media, Inc.
Cover design by Montgomery Media, Inc.
Printed and bound by BookCrafters, Inc.

ASQC Mission: To facilitate continuous improvement and increase customer satisfaction by identifying, communicating, and promoting the use of quality principles, concepts, and technologies; and thereby be recognized throughout the world as the leading authority on, and champion for, quality.

For a free copy of the ASQC Quality Press Publications Catalog, including ASQC membership information, call 800-248-1946.

Printed in the United States of America

 Printed on acid-free recycled paper

 ASQC
Quality Press
611 East Wisconsin Avenue
Milwaukee, Wisconsin 53202

To Joshua, my son,
for your love and playfulness,
and Julie, my daughter,
for your smile and the joy
you have brought into my life

Contents

Preface

This book on organizational reengineering has a dual purpose: to simplify a complex and confusing topic and to present a specific set of techniques that you can apply to your own organization.

This book is for the business professional—the practitioner—who must redesign an organization. This book presents a step-by-step approach to streamlining an organization, making it more responsive to customers, and ultimately, becoming more profitable. Several components explained in this book are used by top consulting firms—only they charge hundreds of thousands of dollars to present them to you.

This book is for the business person who must produce a plan for change that others in the organization will follow. However, it's those "others" who must lead the change. Thus, this book will also provide these "others" with the background necessary to lead that change. For example, it will help the senior executive responsible for improving the efficiency of an organization to understand and apply organizational reengineering. Moreover, this book will help the functional managers who have the responsibility for discrete work areas and are implementing the change. Finally, this book is for managers who have decided to hand the reengineering effort over to a consultant but who want to understand what those consultants do.

This book is not for the theoretician. It does not aim to give you a course in change theory or provide a theoretical dissertation on the reengineering process. Many respected, high-caliber business and psychology academics have written excellent books on change theory. Of course, I have not left out theory completely. Theory is addressed briefly in the beginning of each section—because you should know that the steps presented have an underlying empirical validity and that reengineering has a solid basis in research.

One last note. When I was planning this book, I outlined the idea for several of my peers and my wife. My peers—none are published authors—offered advice that mirrored my wife's, who is an elementary school music teacher: "Keep it simple and easy to follow. If you do, readers will understand what you are telling them, and they can follow your steps." I have tried to follow this advice by keeping the information in this book simple and easy to follow.

Jeffrey Lowenthal, Ph.D.
West Bloomfield, Michigan

Acknowledgments

I have many to thank for their contributions and support for this writing. In particular, I want to recognize Jim Weiner, who during the past five years has been my sounding board, business partner, and friend; Chuck Miller, who suggested that I put all my ideas and concepts into a book; and finally, Kathy Lowenthal, my wife, who taught me that helping people do their best is the most satisfying goal one can pursue and who cheered me on during the months of research, analysis, and writing, never doubting the value of the work.

Special recognition is also extended to Aaron Halabe and Jon Milan, who took the time and effort to read, review, and provide critical input to the manuscript through its various stages, even though tight time frames were imposed. Finally, thanks to my original editor, Susan Westergard, who believed in the book strongly enough to bring the rest of Quality Press on board.

Introduction

In the business world, change has become the norm. The steady, predictable growth of the 1950s, 1960s and 1970s has given way to global marketplace competition, radical technical innovation, limited resources, and major shifts in attitudes about work, employees, and leadership. These changes have no historical precedent. Changes have become more frequent and faster developing, and the business world has become more complex and fluid.

Change is one of the foremost issues, if not the foremost business issue, of our day. *Change* entered the corporate lexicon as a word describing a mixed blessing. On the one hand, change represents growth, opportunity, and innovation; on the other hand, it represents threat, disorientation, and upheaval.

In response to this rapid change, global leaders have offered suggestions to restore growth and profitability. Many view government as the body capable of restoring market leadership. They demand that a new global climate be established, allowing their companies to prosper again. Others point at management leaders of change. Management today not only must do "things right" but also do the "right things."

This book operates from the words of Abraham Lincoln, offered to the nation in a time of crisis and change:

The dogmas of the quiet past will not work in the turbulent future. As our cause is new, so must we think and act anew.

And we are truly in turbulent times. Take, for example, a Russian cosmonaut who spent 313 days in space only to return to a country that no longer existed. Not only was his country gone, but his hometown no longer had the same name as when he left.

The organizations that continuously adapt their bureaucracies, strategies, systems, products, and cultures to the shocks and forces will decimate their competitors. Such organizations will adapt to crises that bedevil others in their industries, maximizing their strengths and developing new strengths as change occurs. These organizations are, or will become, masters of organizational reengineering, an approach that helps an organization adapt to change.

Change is seldom easy. Further, change can neither be rushed nor dragged out. The key is a balance. The intent of this book is to offer a systematic approach—knowledge and techniques—that can help the business professional survive today's turbulence—not only to survive, but to make her or his organization more profitable because of the changes and to become an industry leader.

To meet this goal, this book is divided into five sections. The first section, "Building a Foundation," outlines what an organization is and why change is needed. This is probably the most theoretical section of the book. It discusses change theory, organizational dynamics, and factors that impact an organization. It also provides a brief overview of organizational reengineering and of the reengineering model presented in this book. This first section is important because it provides a foundation for the model that the balance of the book is based on.

The following four sections cover the various phases of the reengineering process—preparing, planning, designing, and evaluating. Each section starts with a general discussion of the topic before providing detailed information about the reengineering steps within that phase of the process. The sixth and final section offers some concluding remarks about organizational reengineering.

Building a Foundation

This first section defines what an organization is and why change is needed. It introduces *organizational reengineering* and outlines the model that is covered in the remaining sections of the book.

CHAPTER 1

Organizations and the Need for Change

Intuitively, we all seem to know what an organization is. However, when a line manager, a senior executive, and a worker on the line are asked to define the term *organizations*, you typically get three very different answers. Thus, this chapter provides a working definition of what an organization is and briefly explores the factors that prompt organizations to change.

WHAT IS AN ORGANIZATION?

An organization can be defined as a structure within which individual and activity contributions are coordinated for the purpose of carrying out planned transactions. Organizations produce something. Typically organizations produce objects, such as toys, or provide a service, such as medical care. However, organizations may produce things less concrete in nature—for example, a school or, our favorite nemesis, the federal government. Schools provide an education for our children and the leaders of tomorrow. Federal agencies such as the Security and Exchange Commission (SEC) regulate businesses so that they behave in a certain way. Although varied in many ways, all organizations have one common characteristic: the goods and services they produce are consumed by portions of society (or at least, the goods and services affect portions of society) outside the organization.

With the previous statement, the definition of an organization can be further enhanced: organizations are contrived structures through which society, or portions of it, obtain things that otherwise could not be obtained at all or could not be obtained as easily or cheaply. Thus, organizations are the intervening elements between what society desires and the satisfaction of those desires.

Organizations do not spontaneously come into existence. It takes hard work to build an organization. For example, a school is more than teachers in classrooms with books and supplies. Schools have to *organize* the teachers, the students, the supplies, and the activities to enable the teachers to educate our children.

To complicate matters, some organizations produce results that are not immediately consumed by the outside world. Some organizations even produce products that are of no interest or use to those outside the organization. An example of this type of organization is the Volume Mailers Association (VMA). The VMA is a group of lettershop owners that meets regularly to discuss trends and new technology available to lettershops.[1] The VMA produces a newsletter, which is the major product of the organization, but it also sponsors meetings and seminars. The VMA consumes its own product. However, society has an interest in how the VMA operates. Federal law prohibits collaboration in price-fixing. So VMA members can discuss new methods in operating their businesses, but they may not discuss pricing of services.

To summarize, an organization is the intervening element between individual contributions and the external environment. This view is illustrated in Figure 1.1.

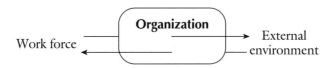

Figure 1.1. Organization as an intervening element.

WHY ORGANIZATIONS EXIST

Organizations are an outgrowth of human limitations. Inevitably, a single individual cannot perform all tasks efficiently and easily. Further, as individuals need more assistance to accomplish a given task, that assistance must be organized. The inevitability of organizations can be best illustrated by an example: Gordon Weiner and his new invention, the *Mouse-Trapper*.

At the beginning

Gordon was a highly skilled worker for Large Corporate America. He was with the company for 22 years and he held different positions. During his career, Gordon worked with plastics, rubber, and metal. In his spare time, Gordon invented gadgets and toys using the skills and materials that he knew. Gordon developed a new and special mousetrap that he felt would have the world beating a path to his door. He was right! Everyone who tried the new mousetrap, the MouseTrapper, wanted one for their family and friends.

Gordon patented his new mousetrap and began building the MouseTrapper in his basement. The production process of the MouseTrapper was simple. It involved an assembly of three plastic parts that are easily molded from plastic pellets (see Figure 1.2). At first, Gordon could work only in the evening and on weekends, but he could still produce about 100 mousetraps a week during that time. The good news was that Gordon sold every trap he made—he even got his wife and kids to help him package the trap. The bad

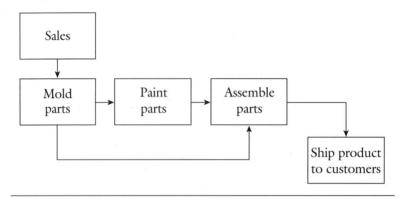

Figure 1.2. Production flow of the MouseTrapper.

news was that the demand quickly became greater than production capacity.

When Gordon was beginning, he had a close neighbor and family friend, Peggy Jamison. Peggy worked as a dental hygienist. However, she wanted to change careers, so Gordon offered her a part-time position. Together, they doubled the production of the MouseTrapper.

The growth period

A regional department store chain found out about the MouseTrapper and offered to buy 500 traps a week for four months. The problem was that Gordon could not pay his bills with a sales volume of only 500 traps per week without his income from Large Corporate America. Thus, Gordon hired three part-time employees to help with the special order, but the demand kept growing.

Gordon received an inquiry from Very Big Retail Chain to supply as many traps as Gordon could produce, up to 4000 units per week. Gordon then quit his job and became the chief executive officer (CEO), president, and treasurer of Mouse Traps Unlimited (MTU). The demand for the trap continued to grow at a rate of 222 percent.

After six months, MTU needed more equipment and space. Peggy, now the shop foreperson, found space at a local technology park, and MTU moved its production and administrative operations there. After 18 months, the demand for the MouseTrapper continued to grow at a rate of 196 percent and Peggy supervised eight full-time employees and nine part-time employees. Gordon continued to add employees and equipment to meet the demand. However, Gordon found he had no time to work on the machines and build the traps—the job he liked the best. Instead, he spent most of his time handling paperwork, hiring people, and performing administrative duties.

The next step

When MTU reached 150 employees, Gordon decided that something had to change. Peggy, while a good plant manager (her newest position), was overwhelmed with the complexity of her new job. So Gordon hired specialists to deal with specific issues. For example, he hired a sales manager to deal with the increase in product demand, a human resource manager to deal with people issues and, finally, an accountant to handle the books and deal with accounts payable and receivable. He also instructed Peggy to hire five individuals to handle the day-to-day operations on the shop floor.

After five years, Gordon was running a successful business that employed several hundred people. In addition, consumer demand for the MouseTrapper was still increasing at a yearly rate of 18 percent. Gordon found that managing a large and successful organization was emotionally and financially rewarding. However, he still noticed several problems. For example, all departments worked well together and shared information; however, it was hard for him, and even for individuals in the factory, to get to know everyone on an individual basis. Further, Gordon had five people reporting to him—Peggy and the heads of the human resources, sales, finance, and legal departments (see Figure 1.3).

The example of MTU shows how one business organization grew and evolved. It illustrates how increases in size lead to the division of labor and task. This characteristic is not unique to any specific industry; it cuts across all industry boundaries. Whether an organization provides a service such as haircutting, or produces a physical product, such as the MouseTrapper, as the work load increases so does the need for an organization.

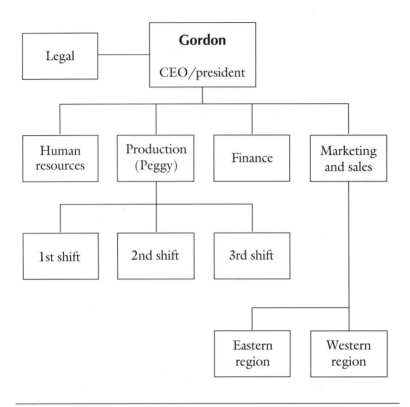

Figure 1.3. Organizational structure at Mouse Traps Unlimited.

FACTORS THAT INFLUENCE ORGANIZATIONS

The factors that influence the growth and character of an organization manifest themselves internally and externally (see Figure 1.4). Internal factors might include the range of products, centralization or decentralization of operations, or divestiture (or acquisition) of other businesses. External factors that influence organizations might include competition, government regulations, or changing economic conditions. These general factors, whether internal or external, are interdependent. In the sections that follow, internal and external factors will be discussed in greater detail.

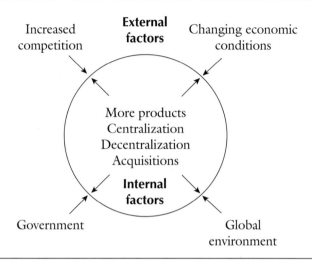

Increased competition   **External factors**   Changing economic conditions

More products
Centralization
Decentralization
Acquisitions
Internal factors

Government   Global environment

Figure 1.4. Internal and external factors that affect organizations.

Internal factors: anticipating change

Every organization has two general categories of internal influences: downward pressures originating within management, and upward pressures arising from the needs and the demands of the members of the organization (see Figure 1.5). Downward pressures are derived from new thinking about workplace relations and new business opportunities. Examples of downward pressures include management directives to centralize or restructure a workplace, or the impact of a new product on an existing production line. Upward pressures include trade-union or employee demands for more money, better working conditions, or the internal enforcement of both federal and state employment labor law.

Internal factors of organizational change have a paradoxical character. The need for change is generated at all levels of the organization, but the responsibility for initiating change rests primarily with management. Further, it is the managers who are often the enemies of change and guardians of established practice.

However, the role of managers as initiators of change is less paradoxical than it seems. Only managers are equipped to take the responsibility for change, and they must take that responsibility for the four following reasons:

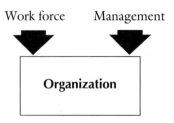

Figure 1.5. Internal pressures affecting organizations.

1. Senior managers have advantages in terms of knowledge:

   • They see the company as a whole.

   • They have a wider range of possible models for change, and they have access to expert resources inside and outside the company to assist them.

2. Managers have the power to make the crucial decisions that set change processes in motion. They can marshal resources and apply them to what they believe will benefit the company.

3. The manager's role is to make the decisions that will secure the company's well-being.

4. If changes in the company's social and political environment (external factors) can affect the organization, it is the job of management to identify these external factors and, if possible, anticipate the changes.

To deal with internal factors of change, managers must learn a special skill. They must scan the internal (and external) environment for the elements of change that will significantly affect the organization. Internally, for example, managers must scan for shifts in the educational levels of employees or in other social influences. Not all internal factors are readily visible; many will even be disguised, but managers must make a conscious effort to identify internal elements of change.

External factors

External factors that influence organizations center on the organization's role in society. Organizations respond to these external factors to maintain their internal stability. There are two general categories of external factors: government and consumers (see Figure 1.6).

Government pressures usually create less anxiety for companies than consumer pressures. Government factors are normally steady or at least predictable. This stability often results from the close relationship that industry builds with government. However, the consumer is far from predictable and, thus, more anxiety provoking.

The history of relations between government and industry has made the government an important player in corporate decision making. For example, antitrust legislation, food and packaging laws, drug safety laws, environmental laws, and automobile safety standards all represent restrictions on industry's freedom of action; they also mark points at which private industry has been made to answer to society's needs. The interplay of government and industry will continue as society's awareness increases.

Consumers constitute the second external influence on organizations. For example, direct actions by groups of activists to change aspects of corporate policy provide a significant new force for change within organizations. Such pressures represent a unique way for corporations to be made accountable for the social consequences of their actions. The result has been, and will continue to be, a greater corporate sensitivity toward developing public concerns. For example, corporate America has increased its sensitivity

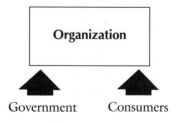

Figure 1.6. External factors affecting organizations.

to several highly visible and often politically based issues such as corporate involvement in defense industries. But more significant is the development of consumer activist groups that judge companies in areas of traditionally internal decision making. Corporations have been scrutinized in areas such as product design and safety and plant location and operation, both of which have formerly been the sacred prerogative of industry. Thus, consumer activism makes organizations more responsive to governmental and consumer influences, which shifts the role of organizations in society.

SUMMARY

The factors that influence an organization today manifest themselves internally and externally. External factors are the most intense and visible, and they receive the most immediate response from management. External pressures will increase as the integration between government and industry evolves. Consumers also influence organizational changes, and their impact is even greater than that of government.

Internal factors for change are driven by the employees of the organization. These employee demands may, in turn, be driven by external influences—for example, laws, regulations, and peer/public pressure. Internal factors are not as readily visible as external factors primarily because internal factors do not manifest with a structured fashion. Internal factors tend to emerge as problems such as declining competitiveness and morale problems among workers.

Whichever factor is pushing the change, the responsibility for identifying it and leading the organization through the change belongs to management. It is management also that must scan the environment for significant changes; managers, particularly top managers, must be sensitive to the changing conditions inside the organization. They must understand what these conditions mean and where they lead. Further, managers must be ready to lead the organization through the change.

Note

1. A *lettershop* is a manufacturing environment that supports direct marketing industries. This type of organization take several types of inserts (for example, letters, brochures, and so on), combines them, and places them in envelopes for mailing. These organizations also sort these mailings to obtain postal discounts.

CHAPTER 2

A Simple Explanation of Change Theory

Change is a slow and, at times, painful process. In the past, inventions and their applications have been ignored by whole populations who had known about them for years. Three examples illustrate this point: first, gunpowder and rifle development; second, the printing press; and third, the facsimile or *fax* machine.

Five hundred years passed between the first known use of gunpowder and the earliest rifles in Europe. In fact, during the following 300 years, so little progress was made in rifle development that Benjamin Franklin suggested to the Continental Congress that the new American army be equipped with the longbow because rifles were inaccurate and gunpowder was hard to obtain. Further, the historical statement, "Don't shoot until you see the whites of their eyes," was made to ensure that no gunpowder was wasted and that every musket shot produced a "kill."

The second historical example is the printing press. The Arabic people had been aware of the technology of printing from the books of the Jewish scholars and the other religious communities they ruled. Yet, they made no use of the printing press until three centuries after Johann Gutenberg's invention. The third historical example is the fax machine, an indispensable tool in most organizations today. Fax machines were invented in the 1950s, but it was not until the 1980s that they became widely accepted. These three historical examples illustrate the slow pace of change in the past.

Before the 1800s, change was localized and sporadic. Change affected a few people in various places or large numbers in one place, but rarely large populations on a global basis. The changes that did occur were so slow or so remote as to be virtually imperceptible. When change occurred at a faster pace, it was typically due to massive social upheavals such as foreign invasions or the overthrow of a regime. This pattern was profoundly altered with the coming of the Industrial Revolution.

Today, change no longer occurs at a slow pace. Many changes can be traced to global communication, the microprocessor, new plastics, and other synthetic materials. Word of new technologies and products travels quickly, via professional meetings, proliferating scientific journals, or global television. Today, we have the capability of communicating simultaneously with nearly every person on the earth, and change continues to evolve.

To understand change, we need to know first the two basic kinds of change: structural and cyclical.

STRUCTURAL CHANGE

Structural change involves a fundamental transformation of some activity or institution. After structural change takes place, the activity or institution is considerably different (and can represent either an improvement or a decline from the previous state). Structural change is not reversible, and it is permanent.

Structural change is radical. For example, the speed of communications increased only slightly as human runners were replaced by messengers on horseback. However, the telegraph and telephone changed the speed of communication dramatically. Today, we have nearly instantaneous communication. In the future, communications will continue to change, not in terms of speed, but in terms of amount and format.

This type of change is irreversible. Communication systems have undergone a permanent transformation and attained a new state. There may be stability in the new state, or there may be a continuing evolution to yet another new state. But the system will not revert to the prior state.

The discovery of the new knowledge and the creation of new technology and equipment make the old system obsolete. Permanent adjustment is required. If an organization does not respond, it will fall behind and be swept under by its competitors.

Structural change may require the dismantling of old institutions, relationships, and procedures and replacement of those institutions with new ones. You cannot expect to move successfully into the future burdened with the baggage of the past.

CYCLICAL CHANGE

Cyclical change, on the other hand, involves a temporary change from a level or state. Over time, cyclical change tends to follow a discernible fluctuation pattern by returning regularly to prior states. An example of cyclical change can be found in the retail industry. Every year around late August to the end of December, retailers hire additional personnel to help with the winter holiday season. This addition of personnel typically requires changes in hiring policy, training, and other administrative tasks. However, after the season is complete, retailers typically return to business as usual.

Cyclical change usually does not cause any irreversible alterations in the structure of the institutions or activities in which they are occurring. Cyclical changes are therefore repeating, nonstructural, and limited; and the required adjustments are temporary.

While the pace of change itself is ever increasing, becoming limitless and infinite, each type of change has its own pattern, with a discernible direction, amount, pace, and duration.

A NEED FOR CHANGE: CONTINUOUS IMPROVEMENT

Physics teaches us that, for a piece of wood to burn, it must be heated to a temperature at which it ignites; then it burns by itself. The initial heating requires energy, but once the wood is ignited, the flame sustains itself and gives off much more energy than was required to start the fire.

A more intense fire than burning wood results from a mixture of aluminum powder and metal oxide. By itself, the mixture is cold and lifeless, but when heated to ignition temperature, it becomes a self-sustaining source of brilliant light and intense heat that cannot be put out by ordinary means. The mixture will burn underwater or in any other environment that would extinguish an ordinary flame. When it burns, the fire is self-sustaining and does not depend on its surroundings for support.

Unfortunately, organizations do not operate like the mixture of aluminum powder and metal oxide; they are not totally self-sustaining. Organizations must rely on both internal and external factors to succeed. Long-term success depends on how well a company can meet and satisfy its customers' shifting demands.

Organizational reengineering is based upon two interacting factors: (1) total customer satisfaction and (2) effective and efficient internal processes. A company's success depends on its ability to satisfy its customers' needs. In turn, this ability depends on how well the organization's internal processes work to meet this external demand. Therefore, the organization succeeds from the inside out: the commitment and dedication of employees to fulfilling customer needs may become the self-sustaining flame that perpetuates success. Competing from the inside out means managing employees, not merely to make them comfortable within a company, but managing them so that the firm can compete in the marketplace.

An organization's success in this respect does not result from quick fixes, simple programs, or management speeches. It starts with the identification of an organization's core competencies, which in turn guide management behavior. This guided management behavior then affects the attitudes and values of all employees toward the realization that competitiveness, internal processes, and effective people management are strongly linked.

The reengineering process is only one method to gain a competitive advantage. Its components are not new or innovative—all have been around for many years, if not decades. What makes the reengineering process so powerful is this blending of the various components into a synergistic whole.

CHAPTER 3

Organizational Reengineering

Business reengineering or *business process reengineering* are terms that have recently entered the business lexicon. Now they are appearing everywhere.

As the terms have has been used across a variety of industries, they have also been grossly misused, and even abused, just like the phrase *new and improved*. Business process reengineering is being slapped onto projects hungry for funding, from traditional automation and systems rebuilding efforts to incremental quality improvement schemes. Additionally, many suppliers have adopted the term to market their same old products and services.

The business world today differs dramatically from the one that existed just a few years ago. For example, we see a rising global competitiveness and a demographically transformed workforce. Further, customer demands have become more intense, for example, customers require an ever-shorter time frame for delivery. Organizational reengineering, business process reengineering, and total quality management are among the strategies some corporations are using to deal with those changes.

Most change processes, such as total quality management, are focused on enhancing products and services to both customers and suppliers. Total quality management requires incremental changes over several years. Those changes are usually small and take place within the current corporate culture. However, some companies have recognized the need for more extensive, almost radical, changes in operations. Organizational and business process reengineering are the processes used to design those radical changes, and they have generated many huge successes.

When a reengineering effort succeeds, companies reap big benefits. For example, a major automobile company reengineered invoice processing and reduced the number of employees in that department by 75 percent with major cost savings. Similarly, a major telecommunications company reengineered part of its service department and cut costs by almost 33 percent.

WHAT IS ORGANIZATIONAL REENGINEERING?

Many business process reengineering firms define their (firm's) product as "a process by which companies become world-class competitors by remaking their information systems, their organizations, their ways of working together, and the means by which they talk with each other and their customers." This is a good starting point for defining organizational reengineering but it is not complete. A historical perspective is needed to more fully understand the term *reengineering*.

A historical look

Exactly how organizational reengineering started is a contentious subject among the industry's professionals. Some claim that the reengineering process started a few years ago as a blending of several methodologies. Others claim that organizational reengineering started in the 1980s, when the American auto industry, battered by

Japanese rivals, began to integrate car design with assembly-line automation. At that time, American automobile manufacturers embraced the ideas of just-in-time (JIT), or delivering supplies just when the factory needs them rather than warehousing inventories, and total quality management, continuously improving the quality of operations and customer service.

Indeed organizational reengineering is several products rolled into one. Organizational reengineering can be compared to a multisymptom cold medication. Just like the various brands of cold medicines, consulting firms that offer reengineering services combine their own ingredients in different formulations. Further, in their marketing strategies, they work to differentiate themselves from each other. However, whatever the mixture of services, reengineering efforts usually have four major components:

1. A greater focus on the organization's customers (both internal and external)

2. A fundamental rethinking of the processes in the organization that lead to improvements in productivity and cycle time (known as process improvement or business process reengineering)

3. A structural reorganization, typically breaking functional hierarchies into crossfunctional teams (team building and organizational development activity)

4. New information and measurement systems, using the latest in technology to drive improved data distribution and decision making (for example, quality and information technology)

When viewed from this perspective, it becomes apparent that the foundation of reengineering has a long history—not just within the past few years, but during the past 100 years.

Process design and the scientific study of work can be traced to the days of Frederick Taylor (1856–1915). The theories of organizational structure and dynamics go back to Henri Fayol (1841–1901), Alfred P. Sloan, Jr. (1875–1966), and Peter Drucker

(1909–   ). Information and measurement systems were addressed by Georg Siemens (1839–1901). Finally, the emphasis on customer focus was established by Robert E. Wood (1879–1969).

This brief history reminds us that the past holds valuable lessons concerning the principles underlying the reengineering process. These lessons from the past can help prevent future problems. Darrel Rigby, author of "The Secret History of Process Reengineering," illustrates the value of one of these historical lessons.[1] His example focuses on a foundation component of reengineering—breaking functional hierarchies into cross-functional teams.

According to Rigby, the battle between the merits of functional-based organizations and process/product-based organizations is well documented. Functional organizations offer the following benefits:

- They maximize development and utilization of specialized skills.

- They offer cost-effective divisions of labor and provide economies of scale in plants and equipment.

- They allow for effective hiring of employees and offer clear career paths for specialized experts.

On the other hand, Rigby says that organizations with cross-functional structures provide better coordination and integration of work, offer quicker response times, and provide for simpler cost controls. This latter type of organization also offers higher levels of employee creativity and greater job satisfaction.

Which type of organizational structure is better? According to Rigby, leading-edge companies vacillate between structure types. They usually start with functional organizations, then shift to a process-focused structure, then a one-or-the-other status, next to a combination of both, and finally start the cycle over. To illustrate his theoretical discussion, Rigby provides the following example of American business' schizophrenia in choosing an organizational type.

During the late 1940s, the predominant choice for organizational structure was the functional one. During the next decade, as organizations pushed decision making down to the lowest levels possible and the hierarchical structure flattened, organizations shifted gears. With this shift, staff size was reduced, and organizations had to focus more on using cross-functional work teams.

In the following decade, the 1960s, there was another shift—this time to situational leadership and structure. In other words, organizations would choose the most appropriate structure—functional or cross-functional—as a situation occurred. Thus, organizations attempted to adopt the best of all worlds—matrix management. Matrix management was the new and innovative structure type of the 1970s. However, matrix management typically resulted in total confusion because managers had extreme difficulty shifting between functional and cross-functional structures on an as-needed basis.

As the cycle continued, the early 1980s brought sharp criticism of the matrix structure, and many large organizations shifted back to a functional structure. However, most managers realized that the functional structure of organizations was not flexible enough for a fluid and dynamic business environment. Thus, it became increasingly clear that the most appropriate organizational structure is the process- or product-based organizational one.

A working definition

Learning from these historical examples, organizational reengineering negates nearly all the premises on which previous organizational structures (functional, matrix, and situational) have been based. Organizational reengineering requires that tasks be compressed and integrated rather than fragmented into specialized and repetitive tasks. Thus, our working definition of organizational reengineering is this:

The fundamental rethinking and redesign of operating processes and organizational structure, focused on the organization's core competencies, to achieve dramatic improvements in organizational performance.

In other words, organizational reengineering is a process by which a company may redesign the way it does business to maximize its core competencies. In turn, this redesign results in dramatically or significantly higher profits, greater customer satisfaction, lower expenses, consolidated activities, and increased productivity. Organizational reengineering redesigns the way work flows through an organization, which often leads to system and infra-structure changes. Further, this process focuses the organization on its core competencies (in addition to cultural aspects of change)—a focus that separates organizational reengineering from business process reengineering.

An organization's *core competencies* are its collective knowledge, including the processes by which it coordinates and integrates diverse production skills and multiple streams of technology. In essence, core competencies are the systems that enable an organization to identify and use—to the best competitive advantage—the knowledge embedded within its organization. (Core competencies are covered further in chapter 7.)

Organizational reengineering involves reorganizing work flows, cutting waste, combining process steps and eliminating repetitive tasks. It will not work within the typical corporate culture because it changes the corporate culture itself. The process sets aside the traditional culture and, in its place, presents a new set of organizational principles by which leaders can rebuild their business. Reengineering strives to break away from the old rules about how organizations are structured and the way they conduct business. Reengineering involves recognizing and rejecting old methods and finding imaginative new ways to accomplish work. New rules will emerge from the redesigned processes to govern the organization. The redesigned processes and the new rules produce a quantum leap in the performance of an organization.

Organizational reengineering does not lead to incremental improvements, which are usually associated with traditional quality improvement programs. Instead, it produces breakthrough improvements in operational and financial performance. Reengineering goes to the heart of the ways in which organizations work. It is not just automating or reautomating existing business processes. It is discarding conventional ways of working and replacing those ways with entirely new ones.

As stated earlier, organizational reengineering centers on the radical redesign of business processes to better meet customer needs through a focus on core competencies and cultural change. It focuses on processes that create something of value for customers, whether they are internal or external. Reengineering can be applied, for example, to new product development processes, which turn an idea into a manufacturable and marketable prototype, or to order fulfillment processes, which begin with the receipt of an order and end when the customer has received and paid for the product. Thus, reengineering examines processes that are cross-functional. Target processes transcend the boundaries between sales, marketing, manufacturing, finance, and research and development. Processes are the neglected orphans of traditional structures. Most companies focus on functions, while processes fall between the cracks.

Organizational reengineering may focus on process redesign, but it doesn't end with process redesign. A radical change in the structure of a process inevitably entails dramatic change in all other aspects of the organization, which include the content and definition of jobs, the shape of organizational structure, and the values and beliefs that people have about what is important to the organization.

In summary, organizational reengineering rethinks the way work is done inside an organization; it does not simply try to improve existing processes. Organizational reengineering changes processes completely, so that they are logical and efficient and driven by an organization's core competencies.

THE REENGINEERING PROCESS: AN OVERVIEW

The reengineering process or model presented in this book provides a holistic approach to the redesign and rebuilding of an organization. It is broader than the model for reengineering business processes, which is only a component of the model presented. This model provides action steps for the strategic, cultural, and technical aspects of reengineering an organization.

Reengineering business processes is not a substitute for strategic direction. For example, reengineering will not help to perfect a process that is flawed. However, when an organization that has a clear strategic direction with a focus on core competencies is reengineered, that organization can better achieve its goals by creatively strengthening and combining customer opportunities.

Note, however, that any changes of processes will be met with resistance inside an organization unless cultural factors such as employee buy-in and job satisfaction are considered as part of the change process. Internal resistance may cause great internal pain and could potentially result in failure of the reengineering effort. Thus, the model strongly emphasizes the preparation of employees for change.

Our reengineering model is divided into four phases, which consist of 13 major steps (see Figure 3.1). The first phase, preparing for change, sets the foundation for future activity. This phase takes a two-pronged approach to change. The first prong involves building understanding and support in management and increasing management awareness of the need for change. These activities provide direction for the reengineering effort and build an internal review and approval process. The second prong prepares for a cultural shift and buy-in by the organization's employees by informing the employees of their role in the upcoming change process.

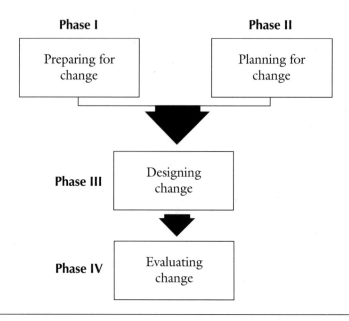

Figure 3.1. Reengineering model overview.

The second phase, planning for change, operates under the assumption that organizations need to plan their future because of the constantly changing marketplace. Any organization that assumes economic conditions, consumer needs and expectations, and competition in the marketplace will be the same two, three, or five years from now is foolhardy and unrealistic. Thus, the planning phase provides a process by which management can envision the future and develop actions needed to operate effectively in that future by building on the organization's core competencies. Planning for change also provides direction and guidelines for the next phase—designing change.

From an operational viewpoint, a process is a bound set of interrelated work activities, each having prescribed inputs and outputs. It has a well-defined beginning and end. A *process* is essentially a method for doing things. The main purpose of a productive process is to create from a set of inputs one or more outputs of greater added value than the inputs.

The third phase, designing change, provides a method to identify, assess, map, and ultimately, redesign business processes. It offers the necessary framework for translating insights about the process being explored into quantum leaps of change. What differentiates the approach presented here from other process improvement or business process reengineering methods are two complementary mapping approaches—flowcharting and integrated flow diagramming—and cultural considerations. These approaches are covered in detail in chapters 10 and 11.

The final phase, evaluating change, provides a means to evaluate the improvement during a predetermined time frame, usually a year, and to develop priorities for the coming years. Specifically, this phase helps determine whether the reengineering effort has been successful and where future efforts should be concentrated.

The balance of this book provides detail on each phase of the reengineering model. Each section begins with a theoretical overview of the phase followed by a detailed discussion of the various reengineering steps.

THE REENGINEERING METHOD: AN OUTLINE

Phase I—Preparing for change

1. Top management explores the reengineering process.

   - Educate management on the reengineering process and the need to change.
   - Create a reengineering steering committee.
   - Develop an initial action plan.

2. Prepare workforce for involvement and change.

Phase II—Planning for change

3. Create a vision, mission, and guiding principles.

   - Identify core competencies.
   - Develop a vision statement.
   - Develop a mission statement.
   - Determine guiding principles.

4. Develop a three- to five-year strategic plan.

   - Conduct a current business review.
   - Determine external environmental factors.
   - Conduct an internal health review.
   - Complete business-as-usual forecasts.
   - Conduct a gap analysis.
   - Develop a three- to five-year strategic plan.

5. Develop yearly operational or breakthrough plans.

   - Develop operational objectives.
   - Organize resources.

- Rank potential changes in order of priority.
- Develop one-year operational plans and budgets.
- Apply and evaluate operational plans.

Phase III—Designing change

6. Identify current business processes.

    - Determine the critical organizational processes.
    - Measure the critical processes.
    - Rate the process performance.
    - Identify opportunities and the process(es) to be reengineered.

7. Establish the scope of the process-mapping project.

    - Identify process stakeholders.
    - Create the project's mission and goals.
    - Structure and select team members.
    - Develop a work plan.

8. Map and analyze the process.

    - Depict the process in a flowchart.
    - Depict the process in an integrated flow diagram.
    - Complete the process-mapping worksheet.
    - Complete the process-constraint analysis.
    - Complete the cultural-factor analysis.

9. Create the ideal process.

    - Describe the ideal process on paper.
    - Compare the current process to the ideal process.
    - Assess the gaps.

10. Test the new process.

- Develop pilot objectives.
- Develop pilot measures.
- Gain agreement and approval from stakeholders.
- Conduct a pilot test of the new process.
- Assess the impact of the pilot test.

11. Implement the new process.

- Develop an implementation action plan.
- Execute the plan.

Phase IV—Evaluating change

12. Review and evaluate progress.

- Evaluate organizational measures.
- Have the steering committee evaluate the results.
- Revise the three- to five-year strategic plan, if necessary.

13. Repeat yearly operational/breakthrough planning cycle (Step 5.0).

Note

1. Rigby, Darrel. "The Secret History of Process Reengineering." *Planning Review* (March/April 1993): 24.

Preparing for Change

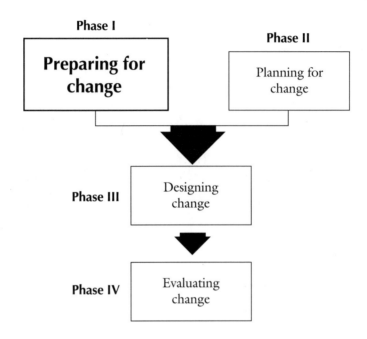

The first phase of organizational reengineering, preparing for change, sets the foundation for future activity. Specifically, this phase involves a two-pronged approach to change. First, it provides the critical mass necessary for any change effort. That is, it builds management understanding and support, and increases awareness of the reengineering process. It also provides direction for the reengineering effort and builds a review and approval process. The second prong provides for a cultural shift. It leads to employee buy-in by educating them about future events and about their role in the upcoming change process.

CHAPTER 4

Setting the Foundation

In early 1983, the book *In Search of Excellence* offered the business community examples of organizational excellence that others could follow.[1] Tom Peters and Robert H. Waterman Jr., authors of the book, had set specific organizational standards and rated a variety of companies against this standard. Three companies—Levi Strauss, Texas Instruments, and Digital Equipment Corporation (DEC)—received high marks and were presented as models of excellence. Less than two years later, *Business Week* carried a cover story titled "Who's Excellent Now?"[2] That story described the difficulties being faced by several companies featured in the Peters and Waterman book.

In the article, Levi Strauss had been caught unprepared when customer tastes changed, Texas Instruments had attempted to become a major manufacturer in home computers, and DEC, resting on the laurels it had won in the development of minicomputers, had missed significant opportunities as the computer market shifted to personal computers (PCs). Specifically, these three companies had failed to live up to their touted excellence.

What many business professionals wanted to know was "What happened?" The critical issue was not that these three companies fell short of the standards that Peters and Waterman had set for them. Instead, they had failed to prepare for and embrace change. In fact, it could be said that all three were resistant to organizational change.

An organization must have a built-in ability to make rapid changes in response to the internal and external environments. Further, it must do so with minimal disruption of services. This ability to transform itself with little, or no, distress and disruption sets the leaders within a particular industry apart from the competition. Organizations that have this transformation ability exhibit two primary characteristics. The first is responsive awareness, or the organization's ability to relate to its changing external environment. The second characteristic is focused flexibility, or the ability of an organization to remain focused while reconfiguring itself to meet the change required by the external environment. These two change characteristics help reduce distress and disruption in the workplace. The process of developing these two characteristics, however, can be time-consuming and expensive.

For example, many American companies are now suffering through the difficult process of downsizing. Many companies view downsizing in a negative light, and they are operating as though their workforce reduction was a one-time activity—that is, they expect that after this round of downsizing is over, they will resume their regular management practices. However, these regular management practices created the need for downsizing. These organizations are not building the ability to adapt to change and, more likely than not, they will have to repeat the downsizing process over and over again until nothing is left to lose. Further, their operations may have been disrupted significantly due to employee fears of lost jobs.

Clearly, many organizations are shortsighted because they are not building the two positive change characteristics of responsive awareness and focused flexibility. Lacking this flexibility, employees experience change as painful, which in turn, causes avoidance behavior that inhibits the change process. However, if properly handled, the pain associated with a change process can be avoided, and organizations will be better able to weather the future storms of change.

THE FALLACY OF PROGRAMMATIC CHANGE

Most change programs don't work because their guiding paradigm is flawed. In this paradigm, a common belief is that change begins with the knowledge and attitudes of individuals. Thus, a successful change effort must begin by changing employee attitudes, which leads to changes in individual behavior. When this change is repeated by many people, the ultimate result will be organizational change.

In a four-year study regarding organizational change, Michael Beer, Russell A. Eisenstat, and Bert Spector found that, while senior managers understand the necessity of change to cope with new competitive realities, they often misunderstand what it takes to bring about change.[3] These senior managers tend to make two assumptions about change. First, they assume that companywide programs such as the development of a mission statement, training courses, and a new performance-appraisal system will suddenly transform an organization. The second assumption, which is driven by the prior assumption, is that employee behavior is changed by altering a company's formal structure and system. Thus, this type of change is like a conversion experience. Once people "get religion," changes in their behavior will surely follow. According to Beer, Eisenstat, and Spector, these two assumptions constitute the fallacy of programmatic change.

An example of this fallacy occurred recently at a Midwest-based publisher. In the early 1990s, a big-six management consulting firm was hired to help streamline the production operations in a more than $100 million division. A divisionwide change effort was announced through a series of town-hall meetings, departmental meetings, and a division newsletter. The change effort was precipitated because the division's profits had been slipping downward during the late 1980s and early 1990s. Further, employees were making serious mistakes that were costing the company tens of thousands of dollars to correct. The solution, as decided by executive management, was to change the way the division operated, and the place to begin was at the top.

The general manager of the division, working with his staff, articulated the division's core competencies, mission and vision statements, and guiding principles. Then, these items were published and distributed to all employees. Further, the manager undertook a divisionwide effort to redesign the work flow and push down change (and accountability and responsibility) throughout the organization. He also initiated a new performance appraisal system.

According to several presentations, the work-flow changes would take between six and 12 months to complete. However, 18 months later, the organization was behaving in the same manner, and serious mistakes were still occurring. What went wrong? Why did this change effort stall?

The answer to the first question is *everything*. Every assumption made by the consulting firm and the divisional leadership staff— about who should lead the change effort, what needed changing, and how to go about precipitating the change—was wrong. In essence, change was attempted by changing individual behavior first and then shifting the organizational structure.

A new paradigm of change, as proposed by Beer, Eisenstat, and Spector, is that individual behavior is shaped by the roles that people play in the organization. Thus, the most effective way to change behavior is to put people into a new role in the organization, which imposes new roles, responsibilities, and relationships on the person. This creates a situation that forces new attitudes and behavior to emerge in the person.

Three interrelated factors are needed to change an organization effectively: *coordination, commitment, and competencies* (see Figure 4.1). Coordination of effort, or teamwork, is especially important if an organization wants to benefit from the existing synergy of employee knowledge and understanding. With proper coordination of effort, an organization can discover cost, quality, and product development opportunities. Commitment to change is

Figure 4.1. Elements of effective change.

essential if management wants cooperation with, and effective implementation of, the changes.

Finally, new *competencies*, such as knowledge of the business as a whole, analytical skills, and interpersonal skills, are required if members of the organization must identify and solve problems as a team. If any of these elements is missing, the change process will break down.

Most business professionals think of training programs as the principle method used to propose change. The problem with training programs is that management generally fails to support the new skills learned in the training session. That is, training programs focus only on competence (skill building). When employees get back on the job, their new skills go unused due to the lack of commitment in an organization, which leads to increased frustration. Thus, many employees view training as a waste of time. This undermines whatever commitment to change a program may have roused in the first place.

On the other hand, the problem with most companywide change programs is their narrow focus. Typically they focus either on commitment or cooperation, rarely on both, and almost never on competence. For example, if senior management develops vision and mission statements that specify teamwork, teams will not spontaneously form, and employees will not necessarily know how to function within the teams to improve coordination.

Another typical problem occurs with the new merit compensation systems that are designed to implement change. Merit programs force managers to differentiate better performers from poorer performers. However, managers are not always trained to carry out skill development (competence) needed to effectively carry out the new system, and thus, the system may actually inhibit cooperation. Corporatewide merit programs have an additional problem. They are designed to cover everyone and everything. Thus, they usually cover nothing particularly well. They are so general and standardized that they don't speak to the day-to-day realities of particular units or employees.

Of course, training or companywide programs are not necessarily inappropriate—both can play a valuable role in supporting an integrated change effort. The key is to have an integrated approach to change, training, and compensation. The previous publisher example had all the right programs—development of divisional direction (vision, mission, and so on), organizational structure redesign, and a new performance appraisal system. However, the various programs were used in isolation. Individually the programs failed to achieve their goals.

When programs are used in isolation, at their best, they are viewed as irrelevant, time-consuming and a current fad that will disappear shortly. At their worst, this lack of integration can inhibit change. In the example of the publisher, the change effort was inhibited because the programs were not integrated. But the question remains: how does an organization carry out effective change?

THE PARADOX

Most individuals believe change efforts should start at the top of the organization and be driven downward. However, according to Beer, Eisenstat, and Spector, most successful change efforts take place at the periphery of the corporation, in a few plants and divisions far from corporate headquarters. In addition, the successful change efforts are led by the general manager of the local unit rather than the CEO or corporate staff people. These findings help explain why in some companies change has very little positive impact, even with wave after wave of program designed to induce change.

In successful organizations, the leaders did not focus on formal structures and systems; instead, they addressed concrete business problems. By aligning employee roles, responsibilities, and relationships, they focused energy for change on the work itself—not on abstractions such as *participation* or *culture*.

Successful managers need to lead a nondirective change process. That is, managers need to create a climate for change and provide the general direction in which the company should move without insisting on specific solutions. The workforce, on the other hand, needs to focus its energies on resolving specific business issues and providing input for directional change based upon its frontline experiences (see Figure 4.2). The next example best illustrates this point.

Located in the Southeast, a first-tier automotive supplier experienced a downward turn in business due to increased overseas competition. The president of the company decided that the organization's core competencies would allow the company to expand into the aerospace and agribusiness markets, and help counterbalance the troubles in the automotive business. The president set the general direction (that is, the two new markets) and allowed the

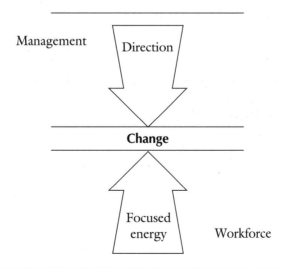

Figure 4.2. Elements of effective change.

organization to build a critical mass for change by preparing the workforce for the changes about to occur.

The formal change started in a small plant in South Carolina, where the plant's management and the workforce together figured out how to change. The president, resisted imposing this successful change on the other parts of the organization (the paradox) and instead simply shared this success with other areas of the company. Shortly, two other plants (Ohio and Pennsylvania) implemented the techniques used at the first plant and demonstrated successful change. Word spread fast, and as other parts of the company started to change, the president realigned the corporate structure and system to the new management practices that had been developed in the periphery. If the president had imposed a structure or a system at the beginning of the change or had attempted to push his own style of management, the tension between these dynamic units and static top management could have caused the change process to break down.

Notes

1. Peters, Tom, and Robert H. Waterman Jr., *In Search of Excellence* (New York: Harper & Row, 1983).

2. "Who's Excellent Now?" *Business Week* (November 5, 1984): 76.

3. Beer, Michael, Russell A. Eisenstat, and Bert Spector. "Why Change Programs Don't Produce Change," *Harvard Business Review* 68 (Nov.–Dec. 1990): 158.

CHAPTER 5

Reengineering Steps

The reengineering effort is often initiated because major challenges, such as lost market share, unhappy customers, declining revenues, and low employee morale, face an organization. However, a reengineering effort may also be initiated due to a leader's vision and understanding of what reengineering can offer. As noted earlier, the first phase of organizational reengineering, the preparation phase (see Figure 5.1), sets the foundation for future activity in two ways:

1. It prepares management to accept and embrace change.
2. It prepares the organization's employees for involvement and change.

STEP 1.0   TOP MANAGEMENT EXPLORES THE REENGINEERING PROCESS.

The organization's top management must set the stage for the entire reengineering process. Thus, if top management does not

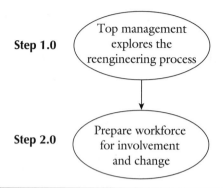

Figure 5.1. Phase I—Preparing for change.

buy into the change process, the effort is bound for failure. Management should follow three substeps to explore the reengineering process.

Step 1.1 Educate management on the reengineering process and the need to change.

Most organizations require significant changes in management philosophy and behavior to survive the fluid and dynamic business environment that exists today. Senior management must become aware of the various phases of reengineering and the potential impact it could have on the organizational structure, culture, and resources. Further, this awareness must occur before any reengineering application is attempted.

Senior management must recognize the need for change. The driving forces can come from feedback generated by a variety of sources. These sources include the following:

- A review of financial projections on profitability/growth
- A review of business trends
- Competitive analysis and benchmarking
- Market trends and requirements
- Market share growth/protection analysis
- Customer demands and satisfaction analysis

Step 1.2 Create a reengineering steering committee.

The creation of a reengineering steering committee (RSC) establishes a high-level management group whose charter and focus is to guide the use and ongoing direction of the reengineering process. This committee ensures that the reengineering effort will receive the attention, focused support, and participation of the highest management levels in an organization. The RSC concentrates on the following issues:

- Development and maintenance of the RSC organization/ charter
- Identification of key opportunities (identified in Phase II— Planning for Change)
- Education and training about reengineering for the organization (Step 1.3 and Phase III—Designing Change)
- Communication and motivation or reward systems
- Identification of major organizational problems, or burning issues
- Coordination of the reengineering application sequence throughout the organization
- Identification of systems to capture gains achieved through the reengineering process
- Collection, analysis, and distribution of reengineering results
- Adaptation of reengineering results into ongoing planning (Phase II—Planning for Change)

While the RSC concentrates on these issues, it must fulfill the following responsibilities:

1. Guide and direct the initial use of the reengineering process.

2. Maintain focus of reengineering efforts on the organization's core competencies and on meeting or exceeding customer requirements (that is, the focus should not be on profit; that comes naturally).

3. Ensure appropriate resource allocation and support for reengineering.

4. Establish guidelines to resolve interdepartmental problems (if they occur).

5. Ensure that the reengineering process does not become an excuse for paperwork.

Step 1.3   Develop an initial action plan.

The RSC must plan for a reengineering effort under clear executive direction and with the shared awareness and understanding of the executive staff. An initial plan is general in scope and context, versus being detailed and very specific. The plan should be general and broad in scope especially when the organization lacks experience in the reengineering process, and provides general guidelines for all future reengineering efforts.

STEP 2.0   PREPARE WORKFORCE FOR INVOLVEMENT AND CHANGE.

This step is similar to step 1.0, but, it involves preparing the entire workforce for the potential changes and informing employees of their role in the effort. More specifically, the RSC educates the workforce about the reengineering process and the need for change.

The workforce preparation rests on four foundation blocks.

1. *Peer consensus.* Most people resist change because it disrupts the ritual and order of their lives. However, one's personal ties with others exert a strong influence. Sharing is a sign of belonging, and few individuals will stand alone. As a result, consensus-building processes based on this natural peer-bonding relationship induce change in organizations.

2. *Two-way trust.* Individuals and groups communicate best in high-trust situations. When communications break down but

individuals trust one another, they are more likely to work though differences that develop and attempt to reestablish communication. Openness about the change process and trust in it influence whether and how change occurs.

3. *Training.* Even if the workforce understands and accepts the upcoming change, it may not have the required skills or the ability to carry out the change. Thus, the work force must be trained in the skills necessary for change.

4. *Adaptability.* The most successful change is that which the work force can easily adapt to the unique circumstances that always develop. Therefore, leaders should only articulate a change idea, or general sense of where the change is headed, and give the employees significant opportunities to adapt the ideas and the resulting processes as they see fit.

PHASE I

Summary

In this first phase of organizational reengineering, preparing for change, the purpose is to provide a foundation for future change activity. Step 1.0 provides the critical mass necessary for any change effort. That is, it builds management understanding and support, and increases awareness of the reengineering process. It also provides direction for the reengineering effort and builds a review and approval process. Step 2.0 provides for a cultural shift. Employees are encouraged to buy into the upcoming change process. This buy-in is critical if the reengineering effort is to avoid stalling or even completely failing.

Planning for Change

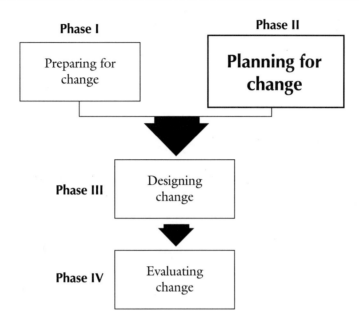

We have assumed in Phase II of the reengineering method, Planning for Change, that organizations need to plan their future because the world is constantly changing. Any organization that assumes economic conditions, consumer needs and expectations, and competition in the marketplace will be the same two, three, or five years from now is foolhardy and unrealistic.

CHAPTER 6

Planning for the Future

Planning is a process by which the management of an organization envisions its future and develops actions needed to achieve that future. Planning for the future has three general levels: forecasting; strategic planning; and operational planning. *Forecasting* attempts to anticipate future trends; it may even use sophisticated models to predict future activity. *Strategic planning* seeks a five- to ten-year vision of the future based on management's forecasts and the existing strengths of the organization. *Operational planning*, already practiced in many organizations, establishes yearly objectives, programs, and budgets. However, operational plans that are developed during a strategic planning process detail how an organization plans to achieve the future described in its strategic plan. Overall, the planning process helps the organization create its future. Phase II of the reengineering model combines the three levels of strategic and operational planning into a sequence of events.

From a reengineering perspective, planning is divided into three major steps.[1]

1. Developing a vision of the future, a supporting mission statement, and guiding principles based on the organization's core competencies (Step 3.0)

2. Deciding how the organization will move toward that desired future in the next three to five years (Step 4.0)

3. Determining the activity each department or division will accomplish during the following year to support the strategic plan (Step 5.0)

History is a great learning tool. If you review the Japanese rise to dominance in several industries during the past 25 years, you see that success doesn't just happen. Instead, people from all levels and functions within the organization work together to achieve the desired results. The Japanese have spent years developing and defining a plan that is strategically focused.

A focused direction is most successful when all members support it. Therefore, the planning process must bring in representatives of all key functional areas, including workers from, for example, manufacturing, human resources, product engineering, purchasing, marketing, and finance. Finally, the executive management of the organization must lead the effort and be an active participant—a top-down approach.

Planning helps an organization answer the following questions:

- Are the organization's mission, vision, and guiding principles clear?

- Have the organization's core competencies been identified, and can they be enhanced?

- Does the organization have the resources and capabilities to meet the future? If not, how will these resources and capabilities be obtained?

When Alice, from the book *Alice in Wonderland*, asked the Cheshire Cat which path to take at the crossroads, the Cat said, "If you don't know where it is that you are going, then any path will take you there." This statement is true for organizations. An organization must know where it is going if it plans to get there. Planning for change is the road map that helps an organization identify its competencies and develop its mission to fit the future environment.

WHY PLAN IN THE FIRST PLACE?

The benefits . . .

Several benefits of the planning process are readily apparent. First, it forces future thinking, highlights new opportunities and threats, and refocuses the organization on its mission. It is a method to stay sharp and focused. Some organizations and their management become so preoccupied with day-to-day issues that they lose all sense of mission and direction.

Second, planning improves organizational performance. History and many great leaders have taught us that attractive visions of the future have great power. A classic example is John F. Kennedy's vision of reaching the moon by the end of the decade—a vision that America achieved two years ahead of schedule. Research studies have consistently shown that vision, planning, and goal setting can positively influence organizational performance and profitability. Further, organizations, both large and small, with strategic plans outperform their competitors who have no long-term plans.

Third, the planning process builds teamwork. Most organizations use a team of people to develop their strategic plan. The team usually includes key staff and leadership with assistance from nonplanning team members. The benefits of this teamwork is improved knowledge of the organization, better communications across levels and programs, improved managerial skills, and increased investment in the organization.

Fourth, planning can help solve major organizational problems in an intentional, coordinated way. It forces an organization to focus on critical problems, choices, and opportunities.

Fifth, planning helps an organization to survive—even flourish—with fewer resources. From the late 1980s to the end of 1993,

America was in a recession that decreased revenue and profit and increased competitive pressures in the marketplace. Faced with problems, organizations had to make difficult choices. The planning process helps organizations think through these difficult choices.

Sixth, planning can help meet shareholders' requirements. With today's pressures from shareholders, leaders sometimes feel less like "movers and shakers" and more like "the moved and the shaken." A strategic plan can be a good communication tool for dealing with shareholders, especially regarding issues of funding. Further, planning can help an organization influence and control the world rather than respond to it.

Finally, planning emphasizes the organization's core competencies. As noted earlier, core competence is the collective learning in the organization, especially the capacity to coordinate diverse production skills and integrate streams of technology. An organization's competitiveness derives from its core competencies. These competencies significantly benefit the products and, in turn, the customers, thus providing barriers to entry for competitors. By planning around, and focusing on, these competencies, an organization strengthens its competitive position and may be provided with increased access to a wide range of markets.

...and the Limitations

Planning is a powerful tool, but it does have its limitations. For example, planning may be inappropriate when a life-threatening problem, such as a severe cash shortage, in the organization needs to be addressed. A strategic plan cannot cure a cash shortage. Organizations in crisis should tackle immediate problems before spending their time and energy on planning. However, planning can assist in identifying those problems if they are hidden.

Finally, the planning process should be aborted and the entire reengineering effort reconsidered if application of the plan is unlikely. Many of my colleagues have had the experience of pouring energy and ideas into a project that was never implemented. Often, this resulted in disillusionment, cynicism, and feelings of powerlessness. It can also lead to an exodus of talent, work slowdowns, or even sabotage. If leaders have no intention of following through on plans, they would be wiser not to plan at all.

The limitations presented are not meant to discourage or deter an organization from developing plans for the future. Planning can be a powerful and practical tool, but it must be used wisely.

BEFORE BEGINNING THE PLANNING PROCESS

Two key points must be remembered during the planning process.

1. Focus on core competencies

Planning must focus on your organization's core competencies. Specifically, identify those skills that are central to the organization's existence and that define what it does best. Planning efforts often derail because a planning team gets bogged down in peripheral issues.

2. Design a planning process that is realistic

Make sure that your organization considers these practical issues.

- The organization's experience with planning. If the organization has never formulated a plan before, seek outside guidance and help with planning.
- The commitment of organizational leaders. The organization's leaders must be committed to the planning effort. If this commitment does not exist, find a way to get it, or abandon the process.
- The time available. Don't design a planning process that will take more time than team members have. Design a planning process that is realistic.
- The leadership available for the planning effort. Appoint, borrow, or hire an individual who understands strategic planning and can guide a group through the planning process. Don't appoint someone who has no planning experience, no concept of the organization, or no experience running a meeting.

- Any technical or political problems that may be encountered. Think ahead in the planning process. If difficult technical issues are anticipated—such as whether to develop a new state-of-the-art process—involve the expertise necessary to make a well-informed decision. If political problems are anticipated—like getting approval from certain groups or reallocating scarce resources—consider involving these people in the process.

Stay focused on the critical issues and be realistic in developing the plan. These are the keys to developing a planning process that fits an organization.

Note

1. Special note regarding the numbering of these three steps. The first two steps are part of the preparation phase; Step 1.0 allows top leadership to explore the reengineering process, and Step 2.0 prepares the workforce for involvement and change.

CHAPTER 7

Reengineering Steps

As noted in chapter 6, the planning phase of the reengineering process consists of three major steps. These steps are displayed in Figure 7.1.

During the first series of tasks (Step 3.0), the organization develops the foundation for the planning activity. This includes the development of the organization's core competencies (Step 3.1), vision (Step 3.2) and mission statements (Step 3.3), and guiding principles (Step 3.4). The organization then examines its existing status and develops a strategic plan (Step 4.0).

An examination of the organization's status (Step 4.1) includes a review of the organization's products, its markets, its customers, and its industry. The process then analyzes the external environment (Step 4.2) and internal capabilities (Step 4.3). The analysis of the external environment includes a review of trends and analysis of activities that affect the company including the competition. An analysis of competitors must include a recognition of their strengths and their weaknesses. Each of these steps is essential. World-class leadership, with total customer satisfaction and the highest

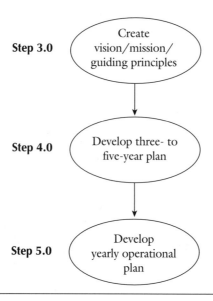

Step 3.0   Create vision/mission/ guiding principles

Step 4.0   Develop three- to five-year plan

Step 5.0   Develop yearly operational plan

Figure 7.1. Phase II reengineering steps.

standards for quality, requires accurate, precise, and documented information to back up the strategic path chosen.

Once the reviews are complete, the organization conducts a detailed analysis of business-as-usual forecasts (Step 4.4) and compares these forecasts against the corporate vision and corporate objectives (Step 4.5). Initially, the comparison will show wide gaps between the forecasts and the visions of its leaders. However, as strategic planning becomes part of an organization's corporate culture, the business-as-usual forecasts and the corporate vision and objectives align. At that stage, the organization's planning is consistent with the corporate direction.

From the gap analysis, a whole series of strategic directions and action programs become apparent (Step 4.6). Planning builds focus and total quality into all aspects of the organization, which helps in organizing corporate resources, setting operational objectives, and planning performance. Only after a strategic plan is developed should the organization develop its yearly operational plans

(Step 5.0), because only then will management know where to steer the organization to achieve its visions.

STEP 3.0 CREATE A VISION, MISSION, AND GUIDING PRINCIPLES.

After identifying the organization's core competencies, the executive and senior leadership will establish the dimensions of the vision for the organization. Specifically, senior leadership chooses the attributes of a best-in-class organization and determines other applications of the organization's core competencies. Next, it groups these attributes and applications, discussing these patterns and relationships. From this discussion emerges a common vision that aligns organizational units and provides a sense of common purpose.

Once a preliminary vision is established, a mission statement can be developed by examining the purpose (driving force) and charter of the organization and by defining what functions the organization performs. In this sense, the mission statement is a list of action statements that becomes a set of guidelines to carry out the vision.

The final step is establishing the organization's value system. It is this value system that guides the behavior of the team carrying out the mission statement.

Step 3.1 Identify core competencies.

Core competency is the collective knowledge possessed by an organization and the process by which diverse production skills are coordinated and multiple streams of technology are integrated. In essence, it is the system that enables an organization to identify and use—to its best competitive advantage—the knowledge embedded within an organization. C. K. Prahalad, professor of corporate strategy and international business at the University of Michigan, is credited with bringing the term to prominence in an article entitled, *The Core Competence of the Corporation*.[1]

The single step of identifying the core competencies of an organization gains the corporation competitive advantage. Core

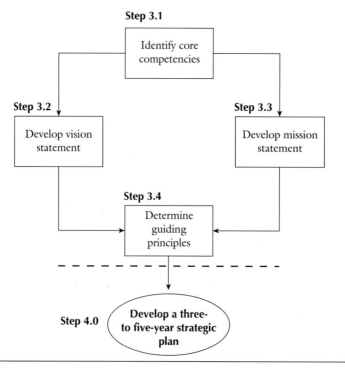

Figure 7.2. Step 3.0. Creating a vision.

competencies are not simply low-cost product differentiation or customer focus; core competencies should be understood as an organization's ability to find and harmonize all the knowledge, skills, and assets that lead to corporate growth in the 1990s and beyond.

> *The diversified corporation is a large tree. The trunk and major limbs are core products, the smaller branches are business units; the leaves, flowers, and fruit are end products. The root system that provides nourishment, sustenance, and stability is the core competence. You can miss the strength of competitors by looking only at their end products, in the same way you miss the strength of the tree if you only look at its leaves.[2]*

Once an organization's management thinks it has identified a core comptency, the competency should be challenged with the following three-prong test.

1. Does the item identified provide potential access to a variety of markets?

2. Does it make significant contribution to benefits of the product as perceived by customers?

3. Does it provide a barrier to entry, or is it difficult for competitors to imitate?

If the answer is yes to all three of the questions, then a core competency has been identified.

Step 3.2 Develop a vision statement.[3]

After the organization's core competencies have been identified, the organization must establish a vision that is based upon those competencies. At the basic level, a vision guides those choices that decide the nature and direction of an organization. It is what an organization wants to be. Specifically, a vision statement articulates the organization's future and sets a focused strategic direction to fulfill customer needs. In developing a vision, the organization must integrate the direction of its future business development (based upon core competencies); its future product and market scope, emphasis, and mix; capability or resource requirements; and its growth (or return) expectations.

Step 3.3 Develop a mission statement.

The mission of an organization explains what business(es) the organization is in, or what function the organization is attempting to fulfill in society or the economy. In formulating its mission, an organization must answer three primary questions: (1) What function does the organization meet when it performs its core competencies? (2) For whom does it perform those core competencies? and (3) How does it use its driving force?

Most organizations answer the first question in terms of the goods and services that they currently produce, but this view is too narrowly focused. It's akin to working with blinders on. As a result of this narrow view, leadership tends to miss new opportunities for growth or appropriate responses to challenges. The best answer to the first question integrates the organization's core competencies and customer needs. Only by doing so can an organization develop new products or services to meet those needs and, in turn, avoid obsolescence or decline.

To answer the "for whom" question, an organization must clearly identify the portion of the potential customer base that is the organization's primary target. In other words, it requires market segmentation. Markets can be segmented in many ways—geographically, financially, or ethnically, for example.

The final question answers how the organization will achieve its mission. This component of the mission statement focuses on the driving force that underlies the organization. The driving force of the organization lies at the heart of its vision. It is the organization's most fundamental building block.

The driving force dictates whether the organization will be a low-cost producer or a technological leader, and whether the organization will revolve around its distribution channels or be product/service driven. Specifically, it is the force that keeps product, market, or business development on track with the vision statement. It causes the organization to accept or reject new product or market opportunities based on its focus.

The literature on strategic planning cites eight basic types of organizations with driving forces used for mission statement formulation.

1. *Product or Service Driven.* A product- or service-driven organization defines its products and services in terms of their common characteristics. When developing new products and services for the customer or when examining products or services to acquire, these common characteristics become the basis for the new products. When attempting to increase revenue and profit, the organization seeks a broader range of customer groups and geographic areas

through which to distribute its products. However, providing products to new customer groups may, over time, require product modifications, extending common product characteristics and, in turn, starting the cycle over. This organization's competitive advantage is in the uniqueness or differentiation of one or more product characteristics.

2. *Market Driven.* This organization recognizes that its highest exploitable competitive edge is in the strength of its relationships with its markets or customer groups. Such an organization is constantly searching for new customer needs, through which it can build strong and well-defined relationships with its customers. The product development, marketing, and market research efforts of market-driven organizations focus on helping customers find their emerging needs and then satisfying those needs with new and innovative products.

3. *Technology Driven.* This type of organization focuses around a body of knowledge or a set of technological capabilities. The organization has the people and the physical resources to push technology to the limits, and it applies this emerging technology in innovative ways to satisfy its customers' existing, emerging, or completely new needs.

The competitive advantage this type of organization enjoys rests in the unique quality or quantity of its technological expertise and its ability to generate a wide range of applications of this technology. It must strive to stay at the forefront of its chosen technology, and it must change the boundaries under which it operates as the technology advances. Its business priorities will depend on the nature of the technological capability and will generally follow this pattern.

- Offer existing product applications of its technology to existing customer groups.
- Offer existing product applications of its technology to new customer groups or new product applications to current customer groups.
- Provide new applications of its technology to new customer groups.

4. *Low-Cost Producer.* Organizations of this type produce standard products; maintain high, steady production levels; and ensure that large volumes of products are readily available. Products are competitive in their features and benefits, but are differentiated by their low price. An organization that is a low-cost producer of goods tends to find that economies of scale are important.

This type of organization has a set of production capabilities to create products or services at the lowest possible cost compared with its competitors' offerings. It uses its knowledge of advances in process technology or production methods to stay ahead of competitors and to avoid obsolescence of its production capabilities. This type of organization targets markets or customer groups where price is the principal buying motive.

5. *Operations Driven.* An operations-driven organization has a set of capabilities—physical, human, and technical—that it uses in a variety of combinations to produce a wide range of products or services. The organization's competitive advantage stems from these capabilities and the ability to use them flexibly by allocating the appropriate mix of capabilities to deliver specific products or services.

The features and benefits of the products or services are set by the customers' specifications and the nature of the organization's capabilities. Turnaround time and low costs may be important competitive factors. An operations-driven organization will target markets selectively based on its particular mix of capabilities. Customers for new products or services may vary considerably from those of the core business.

6. *Method of Distribution/Sale.* An organization pursuing a method-of-distribution/sale driving force has distribution and sales capabilities and the physical and human resources necessary to take full advantage of them. This results in the ability to provide a variety of products or services with a particular competitive advantage.

To gain maximum advantage from its existing distribution and sales capabilities, this organization may choose to handle compatible products that it does not produce. This type of organization may also seek to develop or find other distribution or sales channels that are similar in nature to its current capabilities. The priorities of a distribution/sales-driven organization are the following:

- To improve its position in current markets by building on its uniqueness or low-cost position
- To offer new products to current markets

7. *Natural Resources.* This type of organization owns or controls a significant natural resource. It may possess the capability to process that natural resource into usable forms. However, the organization's competitive advantage rests in the quality, quantity, location, or form of the natural resources themselves. The organization seeks to maintain its advantage in one or more of these areas by adding to the natural resource ownership or control as necessary. It may also seek ownership or control of other natural resources that may be used as substitutes.

This type of organization may produce a variety of products or services from the resource, or it may license or use joint ventures to develop new products or produce the products it sells. Its primary strategy is to control its resource for future exploitation.

8. *Profit/Return on Investment.* Every organization must produce some return on the capital it invests, and it must take care not to confuse that return with profit as a measure of performance. Further, every business manages its operations with profit uppermost in mind, but this does not mean that such an organization uses profit/return on investment as its foundation. However, some organizations do decide that the sole reason for entering into, or staying in, a certain line of business is capital return and profit. If a division of such an organization falls short of its financially oriented strategic criteria, the division is often sold, deemphasized, or dismantled. Typically, organizations with this driving force purchase businesses rather than develop new products or customers. This organization's focus is purely financial.

The strategic planning team must select the driving forces that are most applicable to the organization (usually an organization has more than one) and rank the driving forces in order of importance. A consensus on the most important driving forces will enable the planning team to allocate resources more easily.

Developing a mission statement can be a difficult and time-consuming task, but one that the planning team must complete before moving on. A mission statement provides a valuable management tool to an organization and an invaluable tool for measuring the organization's reengineering efforts.

Step 3.4   Determine guiding principles.
This step involves the examination of the guiding principles of the leadership group and those of the organization.

Individual guiding principles. The personal guiding principles of the leaders, including the members of the planning team, must be examined. Such principles, especially those of the leaders, often become part of the organization's culture. For example, a leader whose behavior (guiding principle) promotes employee empowerment will have a different impact than a leader with authoritarian behavior.

Organizational guiding principles. The guiding principles of the organization must be identified because any plan inconsistent with existing organizational principles is unlikely to succeed. Specifically, the organization's guiding principles include assumptions about the way things work and the way decisions are made. These assumptions must be examined in terms of their current validity and relevance, or the organization will continue to assume that they are true and operate accordingly.

STEP 4.0   DEVELOP A THREE- TO FIVE-YEAR STRATEGIC PLAN.

In this step, the team uses the information and lessons learned from the prior steps—the analysis of the organization's core competencies, vision and mission formulation, and development of guiding principles—to develop a plan that encompasses the next three to five years. It is at this point that the organization makes the commitment to the future (see Figure 7.3).

Step 4.1   Conduct a current business review.
No organization exists in a vacuum. Demographics, value shifts, world markets, environmental regulations, legal restraints, and social responsibilities are just some environmental characteristics

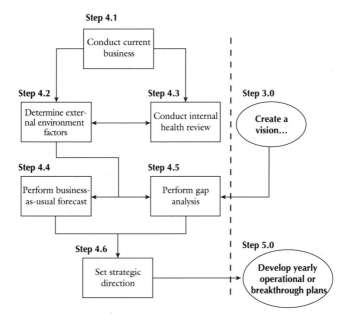

Figure 7.3. Step 4.0. Developing a three- to five-year strategic plan.

that cannot be ignored. The purpose of this step (and Steps 4.2 and 4.3) is to ensure that the preliminary vision established in Step 4.2 is in line with the real world. Thus, data about the entire organization must be pulled together and a snapshot of the organization presented. Collection and analysis of these data will help the executive and senior leadership to understand where the organization is and what it should be. This process also highlights organizational data that are incomplete or nonexistent.

The process of synthesizing data collected from many sources and reviewing them under scrutiny often results in a more intense and complete effort to gather further information. Thus, the organization is forced to upgrade its knowledge base and its assumptions about itself.

Step 4.2 Determine external environmental factors.

The organization can identify improvement opportunities by documenting the strength of the organization and the strength of its competitors. A clearer picture of competitors and customer needs and expectations emerge from this analysis. This process can point to products and services that respond to customer desires and provide an advantage in the marketplace. This analysis can be simplified through benchmarking an organization and its competitors (or the organization's best-in-class competition).

Step 4.3 Conduct an internal health review.
In Step 4.1, the organization identified a macroview of itself. However, it must also assess the readiness of the organization for change before embarking upon the reengineering process. Usually this is accomplished by surveying employees (and management) to determine current levels of employee morale and confidence in the management of the organization. If the workforce is divided due to a lack of target focus, a high level of distrust, or a lack of confidence in the management, reengineering efforts will be resisted.

Further the organization needs to identify employee and management concerns (and complaints) about the organization. With this information, the internal barriers to the success of a reengineering process can be identified, and both preventive and contingent actions can be taken to help the entire workforce accept and use the reengineering process.

Step 4.4 Complete business-as-usual forecasts.
A *business-as-usual forecast* is developed under the assumption that the organization is neither ready nor willing to change. Here, the leadership team creates forecasts that reflect the future conditions of the organization if no changes occur.

Step 4.5 Complete a gap analysis.
A *gap analysis* is a comparison of (1) the internal, external, and business-as-usual reviews (a strategic profile) with (2) the vision and mission statements (direction). If a substantial discrepancy between the profile and the organization's direction exists, the planning team needs to either revisit the vision and mission statements or shift the direction of the organization toward the attainment of the vision and the mission.

Step 4.6 Develop a three- to five-year strategic plan.
The leadership team uses the information developed in the prior steps to formulate this strategic plan. Then the plan is summarized, and the summary undergoes an organizational review.

During the formulation of the plan, a planning approach is selected. A planning approach enables the organization to identify and evaluate alternative futures and develop a total strategy for moving toward the organization's desired future. The team can select from three basic planning approaches:

- Scenario approach
- Critical-issues approach
- Goal approach

While approaches may be used individually or in combination, a single approach is recommended to organize the planning process. Any of the three approaches are acceptable, but most literature on strategic planning suggests the goal approach.

Scenario approach

The scenario approach begins by outlining one or more pictures of the future. To do this, members of the planning team review the material from the previous steps. Next they are provided with the following instructions:

Imagine that it is three years in the future, and our organization has been redesigned in a very exciting way. Imagine that you are a newspaper reporter who is writing a story about our organization and that you have thoroughly reviewed the organization's mission, services, products, personnel, finances, and so on. Describe the organization in a few phrases or with a picture.

After making notes, each planning team member takes about 10 minutes to describe the best possible future he or she can imagine for the organization. The meeting leader records the components of each view. At the end of the meeting, the similarities and differences between scenarios are listed and discussed.

A second meeting is scheduled, and there, each scenario is rated on several factors such as fit to vision, mission, and so on. Then the advantages and disadvantages of each scenario are listed. By the end of the meeting, the scenario that is the most promising is selected. Finally, the selected scenario is tested and refined. This strategy has several advantages.

- It is quick.
- It holds people's interest.
- It uses "big picture" thinking and focuses on major shifts in emphasis or direction.

Critical-issues approach

With the second approach, the planning team sequences the critical issues from prior steps in some logical order. Possible solutions to each issue are listed, and the best solution is chosen. Sometimes prior decisions must be revised in light of later decisions, but the approach works. After resolving the major issues, the planning team reviews the organization's overall strategy to ensure that it is sound.

Goal approach

The third approach is to select the organization's major goals or targets for coming years and then choose the best strategy for reaching each goal. This approach focuses on a few major goals or targets that drive the organization—for example, market share or profitability. However, the goals should be directly linked to the organization's core competencies. Strategies are developed to reach each goal, and detailed plans are formulated for accomplishing each strategy.

After the planning approach is selected and the strategic plan is developed, an overview of the plan is communicated down through intervening levels of management and the general employee population, with requests for contribution and feedback. Special attention is given to these responses. The feedback is consolidated, and then the full multiyear plan is developed in detail for the organization.

STEP 5.0   DEVELOP YEARLY OPERATIONAL OR BREAKTHROUGH PLANS.

In operational planning, the organization focuses on short-term or critical breakthrough areas needed for significant product or service improvements. The purpose of operational planning is to clarify the vision of the organization and to align this vision with the methods by which the vision will be achieved (see Figure 7.4). Further, this type of planning provides the structure for monitoring and assessing progress toward the organization's vision.

Yearly operational plans ensure that the organization is in alignment down to the departmental level. They give the leadership team a tool for assessing departmental activity and monitoring this activity on a monthly, quarterly, and annual basis. They also allow individual leaders to assess their area's activities for alignment with corporate activities.

Step 5.1   Develop operational objectives.

Long-range plans standing alone will not magically materialize. Achieving visions requires a transformation of the visions and the missions of the organization into action. Managers at the

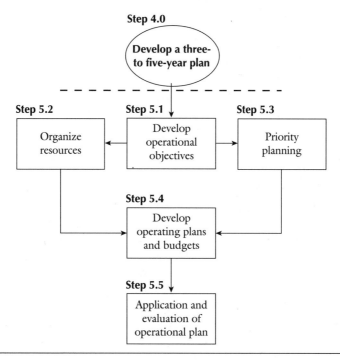

Figure 7.4. Step 5.0. Yearly operational planning.

departmental level need to establish operational goals that they will accomplish within the next 12 months. Moreover, these goals must support the larger, longer-term plan. Finally, these goals should be based upon key results areas, and they need to be measurable and observable.

Step 5.2 Organize resources.

In most organizations, resources are limited and have to be appropriately allocated. Thus, the organization must analyze its existing resources and the resources needed to meet objectives. Then, it must align the two.

Step 5.3 Rank potential changes in order of priority.

The organization has articulated a vision leading to a mission statement; developed an internal health review, an external environmental review, and operational plans; and aligned its resources with the visions and goal. This whole sequence, and the communications with employees and management, should identify areas for system and process changes that now must be ranked. This ranking points the organization toward actions that will overcome the barriers and interference it will encounter in meeting its vision.

Step 5.4 Develop one-year operational plans and budgets.

Each leader reviews the department's objectives and then develops (both individually and in discussion with his or her manager and employees) the short-term plans by which the department will contribute to the achievement of those objectives. No objectives should be set without corresponding means to support them and measures to assess their achievement. This process should result in an exchange up and down the organizational structure.

At the same time, the manager decides the measures by which the results and the process used to achieve those results will be monitored. This information should be clearly disclosed and charted to make it visible. The inputs from various leaders are collected and made visible in an organizationwide chart that depicts the contributions to be made from every group and department.

Step 5.5   Apply and evaluate operational plans.

After the preceding analysis is completed, individual managers initiate action according to the operational plans. This may or may not involve the implementation of a complete reengineering project. It will not if you are satisfied with the results you get from your Phase-II analysis. However, if your organization is like most, reengineering of some, or all, of its processes may be needed. Hence, you will need to proceed to Phase III, Designing Change, which also requires an audit of the results achieved and the processes followed by each leader. Furthermore, progress should usually be checked by the individual leader at least monthly and reviewed by the leadership team quarterly.

Notes

1. Prahalad, C. K. "The Core Competence of the Corporation." *Harvard Business Review* (May–June 1990): 79.

2. Ibid.: 82.

3. Significant portions of Step 3.2 and Step 3.3 on pages 65–69 have been excerpted from the book *Vision in Action: Putting a Winning Strategy to Work* by Benjamin B. Tregoe, John W. Zimmerman, Ronald A. Smith, and Peter M. Tobia (New York; Fireside Books/Simon & Schuster, 1989). Kepner-Tregoe, Inc. is a management consulting firm with headquarters in Princeton, New Jersey.

PHASE II

Summary

The steps outlined in this chapter should assist an organization in developing strategic and operational plans. Here are the most important points to remember about strategic planning.

- Do strategic planning properly by making it highly customer focused.

- Identify your organization's core competencies by defining what your organization does best. Planning blends what the organization does best with customer requirements to maximize market share, productivity, and profitability.

- View planning as a way of thinking—an ongoing process. A plan is never perfect or complete.

- Keep the planning simple and manageable.

- Involve the organizational leaders. Don't give the task of planning to a support staff or a consultant.

- Emphasize creativity, innovation, and imagination rather than blindly following a set of planning steps.

- Don't adopt strategies without carefully considering how they will be carried out and what their results will be.

- Don't view planning as an end in itself. It is simply a tool to help an organization accomplish its mission.

Designing Change

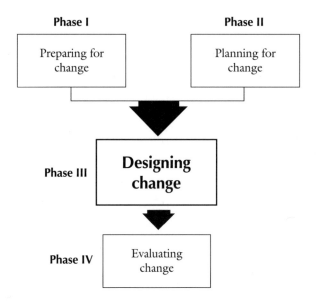

The purpose of this section is to provide a method to identify, assess, map, and ultimately, redesign business processes. This section offers a framework for gaining insights into processes and translating those insights into quantum leaps of change. This approach differs from other process improvement or business process reengineering methods because it offers two complementary mapping approaches—flowcharting and integrated flow diagramming—and it considers the culture in which the process operates.

C H A P T E R   8

Defining a Process

WHAT IS A PROCESS?

In its simplest form, a process can be defined as a bound set of inter-related work activities, each having prescribed inputs and outputs. Inputs, which can be material, equipment, other tangible objects, or various kinds of information, are converted by a series of activities into an output that is provided to a recipient (see Figure 8.1).

The recipient can be either an external or internal customer. An external customer is a person or organization that pays for the service or products received. An internal customer can be a department, a group (in case of an internal operation), or some other processing equipment and machinery. A recipient can also be a location where the process's outputs are stored for future use (for example, a warehouse).

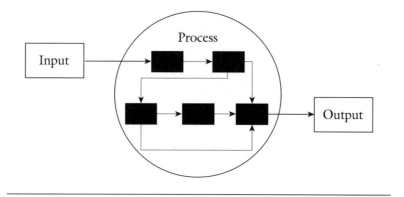

Figure 8.1. A simple process.

A process has a well-defined beginning and end. Further, processes typically cut across functional boundaries in an organization (see Figure 8.2).

This simplified definition of a process needs expansion. From a reengineering perspective, defining a process as the transformation of input to output does not fully explain what a process is or what process components are. Thus, a process can be further defined by its four key functions:

1. Endpoints
2. Transformations
3. Feedback
4. Repeatability

Endpoints

The *endpoints* of a process can be defined as its inputs and outputs. Specifically, endpoints can be broken into four categories:

1. Inputs
2. Outputs

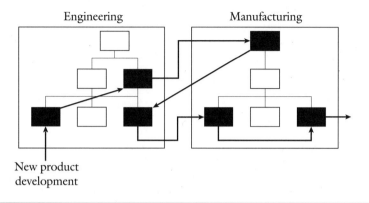

Engineering   Manufacturing

New product
development

Figure 8.2. A crossfunctional process.

3. Customers

4. Catalyst event

As stated earlier, *inputs* to a process can be equipment, materials, methods, or the environment necessary to produce the products and services of the process. At the other end of the process are the outputs. *Outputs* are the products or services produced by the process. The third type of endpoint is customers. *Customers* are the users of the products or services produced by the process. Customers can be either internal, such as a department or group, or external to the organization. Customers are the ultimate judges of the quality of the process outputs. The primary customer is the most important customer for any product or service. Further, the primary customer is the principal reason that the process exists and the end boundary of the process. The final endpoint type is the *catalyst event*. While a catalyst event can be classified as an input, it should be seen as an independent endpoint. It is the single event that signals the beginning of the process. The catalyst establishes the initial boundary of the process.

Transformations

The *transformation* function of a process can be classified into three categories.

1. Physical
2. Locational
3. Transactional

A *physical transformation* changes some tangible item, such as raw or semifinished material, into another state. For example, the act of melting down pellets, injecting the melted plastic into a mold, and producing the MouseTrapper described in chapter 1 is a physical transformation. The assembly of a final product from various components, such as the assembly of a computer from the metal casing, electronic circuitry, and connectors, is also a physical transformation.

Closely related to a physical transformation is a *locational transformation*. A locational transformation also changes physical items. However, locational transformation changes the location of objects or materials and does not change the materials in any other physical manner. In our earlier example, the movement of plastic pellets from the warehouse to the shop floor or the movement of the final product from the shop floor into the storage or shipping area are locational transformations.

The third type of transformation, *transactional,* involves the modification of nontangible items. These nontangible items include the electronic movement of money in banks, the sales of stock by stockbrokers, or the assembly of marketing research data by advertisers. Here, the primary input item is information or data. The transformation process could, thus, involve the modification of data. For example, the output from marketing surveys may be data that have been converted into meaningful information, such as a customer-satisfaction analysis. Data processing, financial planning, and production control typically incorporate this type of transformation.

Most business processes contain at least one, and often two or more, transformation types. In our primary example of the injection molder who makes the MouseTrapper, the production process includes all three types. The physical transformation includes the change from plastic pellets to the product. The locational transformation would be the movement of the final product to shipping for distribution. Finally, the transactional transformation occurs in the creation of the shipping documents and the invoice for billing.

Feedback

Feedback involves communication and evaluation channels by which the transformation activities are modified, or corrected, to maintain the desired attributes of the output. Every process requires feedback to regulate its output. Feedback can take many forms. It can occur as information from the output side of the process or from checkpoints inside the conversion processes. Feedback can also take the form of economic information, such as gross sales revenue, which is used to evaluate the operation. Feedback ensures that the process is effective, efficient, and achieving its desired output. Feedback can be divided into five categories.

1. Customer needs and expectations
2. Specific customer targets
3. The voice of the customer
4. Specific process targets
5. The voice of the process

The first three categories of feedback involve information from the output of the process. *Customer needs and expectations* are those attributes of the process output—for example, products and services—that the customer requires. *Specific customer targets* are the translation of customer needs and expectations into specific and quantifiable characteristics that can be used to assess the quality of the product or service. The *voice of the customer* is the feedback mechanism by which the customers' satisfaction with the product or service can be measured. The voice of the customer should be used to learn if the process output is meeting customer needs and expectations.

The last two categories of feedback involve information from within the process. *Specific process targets* are those objectives, goals, and targets that the process must achieve to meet the needs and expectations of the customer. These targets represent a direct translation of the specific customer targets. The *voice of the process* provides information by which the process can be measured and examined against the specific process targets. One important distinction: The voice of the process provides information before the customer receives the product or service.

Repeatability

The final characteristic of the process, *repeatability*, implies that a process is or can be executed regularly in the same manner with the same output. Some processes are continuous, while other operate cyclically or intermittently. The process of assembling cars on a production line is a continuous process. Building custom cabinets for new houses is an intermittent process. But, whether a process is continuous or intermittent, it must be repeatable.

PROCESS CHARACTERISTICS

While the prior section explores the four key functions of a process, this section will briefly examine process characteristics.[1] Whether a process involves transformations of a physical, locational, or transactional nature, it has 10 common characteristics.

1. Clearly defined ownership
2. Boundaries
3. Capacity
4. Documentation
5. Control points
6. Effectiveness
7. Efficiency
8. Adaptability

9. Measurements

10. Corrective action

Clearly defined ownership

Traditionally, the ownership of physical and locational processes has been clear and explicit. The process owner was the departmental manager. This manager understood the organizational mission and the process's output, and he or she had personal responsibility and accountability for the process and its output. In addition, the manager's performance was judged by quantifiable standards, such as cost, schedule, and quality. In recent years, *process ownership* has gradually shifted toward empowered work groups and self-directed work teams. And in these teams, employees are assuming some traditional roles of management. However, the basic ideas remain the same: the process owner, whether an individual or a team, is responsible for yield, cost, quality, and schedule; the process owner must manage the process to the targets set on this standard; and the process owner has the authority to change the process to maintain its desired outputs.

Boundaries

Boundaries are the beginning and end of a process. Physical and locational processes have clearly defined boundaries. The final output from and the input(s) required by these processes are clear and unambiguous. However, the boundaries of transactional processes are harder to identify. Further, output specifications for transactional processes may not truly reflect customer requirements, and input specifications may not achieve the desired output specifications with the existing processes. A lack of understanding about the input specifications and the output specifications is common in many business processes. But in a well-managed transactional process, specification problems are minimized through conscious effort aimed at classifying the work product as it proceeds from one operation to another. Thus, the boundaries of a well-managed process are well-defined and controlled.

Capacity

Capacity is the output rate of the process. Capacity is usually expressed in terms of design, or theoretical, capacity and effective capacity. Thus, design capacity is stated without consideration for such matters as equipment reliability, maintenance, or personnel factors such as learning curves, absenteeism, illness, and so on. These considerations, when allowed for, enable effective capacity to be calculated.

Documentation

Documentation is a detailed record of work flow in processes. Documentation can be written in great detail, or it can be a collection of various bits of data. Further, it provides a permanent record of the physical transformation taking place in a production process. Documentation provides a reference point from which the repeatability of a process can be measured, and it provides a baseline from which any changes can be measured. Finally, documentation serves as both a training and reference aid for the personnel involved in the process.

Various types of documents exist. Typical documents include process flowcharts, assembly drawings, and routings. Process flowcharts graphically describe the sequence of operations in the process. Assembly drawings show how a product is constructed. Routings describe operational steps that accompany the process flowchart.

Control points

Control points regulate the quality of work or provide feedback. Control points are established to manage the natural variation that occurs in physical processes.

Effectiveness

Effectiveness differs from feedback in that effectiveness measures feedback against process goals. Effectiveness is best assessed by measurement, both internal and external. External effectiveness measures must reflect customer requirements. Internal effectiveness measurements must reflect both external and internal customer requirements. Thus, internal effectiveness measurements should proceed from the external boundary (for example, customer requirements) to the starting boundary of the process. Integrated flow diagrams that reflect established requirements are useful for measuring effectiveness (see chapter 11).

Ineffectiveness is often easier to identify than effectiveness. These are some symptoms that suggest an ineffective process.

- Customer complaints
- Inconsistent output quality
- Lack of awareness of output quality
- Absence of a corrective-action system
- Lack of interest in the customer
- Long response times in correcting problems

Efficiency

Efficiency is a measure of the output against the resources required to achieve that output. It reflects how productive the internal operations are and how effectively resources are used in the process. A traditional measure of efficiency is the ratio of output to the capacity of a process.

Inefficiency, like ineffectiveness, is easier to identify than efficiency. These are some symptoms of inefficiency.

- Multiple off-line inspections
- Redundant, unnecessary, or nonvalue-added activities
- Corrective actions such as rework and reconciliation
- Supplier problems (for example, poor quality or late deliveries)
- Excessive costs of value-added activities (for example, high production costs)

Adaptability

Adaptability refers to the ability of the process to adjust to change—either technological or output changes. Further, adaptability encompasses the response of a process to changing conditions such as output requirements, internal constraints, and input quality. A process is adaptable if the process can be changed to meet new requirements without significant modifications. An adaptable process may require some work flow, personnel, and equipment changes when a process change is needed, but the process should remain largely intact. Processes that lack adaptability tend to be limited in nature. The limitations may involve equipment capability, such as capacity, throughput, and cycle times, or human aspects such as skills, flexibility, resistance to change, and other human factors.

Measurements

Measurements provide a statistical basis for controlling the flow of work and managing variation. In other words, they provide a basis for feedback. Continuous measurements are inherent in any well-managed process because they verify that the product will meet specifications. Moreover, continuous measurement allows the process to adapt to the natural variations that occur in processes. Most organizations that previously relied only on end-of-line measurements, or final quality controls, now find that approach costly in terms of scrap and rework. Measurements and analysis of measurements by statistical techniques, such as Pareto analysis and variation charts, are useful for managing repetitive operations.

Organizations also need to measure products against the requirements of the process without removing the product from the process. A process that is not susceptible to measurement is exceedingly difficult to control. However, all products are measurable; thus, all processes are measurable. The trick is to pick the right characteristics to measure.

Corrective Action

Corrective action is the action required to correct for natural variations in a process. In a well-designed and -managed process, internal feedback from measurements at one or more control points identifies the need for corrective action before subquality products are produced. The process is quickly adjusted to correct for the variations, and the process's effectiveness and efficiency do not suffer despite the natural variations. Feedback and corrective action are the heart of process control; without them, the process loses its repeatability, quality, and consistency.

ANOTHER VIEW

Earlier, a process was defined as the transformation of an input to an output. A process can also be categorized by its operational environment. The two categories of operating environment are manufacturing and service organizations. Both use the same three transformation types. However, service-organization processes have five features that distinguish them from manufacturing processes.

1. *Degree of customer contact.* Processes in service organizations vary in degree of customer contact. Contact ranges from virtually none, such as in the processing of life insurance applications, to complete contact, such as in a dental treatment. In contrast, traditional manufacturing processes have little or no contact with the customer.

2. *Intangibility.* Often, service cannot be touched or felt by the customer. An example is the processing, and paying, of a medical bill by a health insurer.

3. *Immediacy.* The catalyst event of a service organization process occurs at the point of customer contact. The process starts immediately and sometimes includes direct customer participation. An example is the customer who is returning an item to a store for a cash refund. Here, the catalyst event is the customer requesting a refund. The process starts immediately, and the output is the cash returned.

4. *Nonaccumulation.* Since service is an experience, rather than a product, output from service processes cannot be accumulated or inventoried.

5. *Labor intensiveness.* Service processes are accomplished by a wide range of people, capital, and automation. However, service

Table 8.1. Differences between service and manufacturing processes.

Characteristic	Service	Manufacturing
Ownership	Tends to be ambiguous or has multiple owners	Usually clearly defined
Boundaries	Often unclear, fuzzy	Clearly defined
Control points	Often nonexistent	Clearly established and defined
Measurement	Often nonexistent, hard to define	Easy to define and manage
Corrective action	Usually done reactively	Performed during and external to the process

processes tend to be more labor intensive than manufacturing processes. Examples of labor-intensive processes include legal, retail, hotel, and hospital services.

Note that both manufacturing and service processes contain the 10 characteristics outlined earlier. Typically, though, the thoroughness and attention paid to these 10 characteristics vary depending on the environment. Table 8.1 summarizes some differences between processes in manufacturing and service environments.

Note

1. A comprehensive source on process management is Eugene Melan, *Process Management: Methods for Improving Products and Service*. (Milwaukee, Wisc.: ASQC Quality Press,) 1993.

CHAPTER 9

Reengineering Steps Part 1

Because the design phase of the reengineering model has so many facets, the steps will be divided between several chapters. This chapter will provide an overview of the design phase and introduce the first reengineering steps: Step 6.0—identifying current business processes, and Step 7.0—establishing the scope of the mapping project. Chapter 10 will cover the first part of Step 8.0, in which a process is mapped and analyzed. Chapters 11 and 12 will cover more of Step 8.0, the introduction of integrated flow diagraming, process-constraint analysis, and cultural-factor analysis. Chapter 12 also outlines the final steps in the design phase: Step 9.0—creating the ideal process, Step 10.0—testing the new process, and Step 11.0—implementing the new process.

OVERVIEW

In preparing and planning for change, the reengineering process addressed the organization as a whole. That is, it prepared the employees of the organization regarding the upcoming change and established an RSC. It also guided the top leadership of the organization through a planning process, developing core competencies and strategic and operational plans. All this activity was global in nature. It involved all parts of the organization. The designing phase, however, focuses more on specific areas, such as accounts payable, shipping and receiving, or a manufacturing process. Of course, the focused effort will still have a wide-range effect. As stated earlier, processes cut across functional lines. Thus, any process reengineering effort will affect many aspects of the organization (see Figure 9.1).

To begin this phase, a project leader needs to be identified and selected. This individual has the responsibility to guide a team, guide those persons who will actually design the change, and be the liaison between the design team and the RSC. The first activity of the team is to identify the critical organizational processes (Step 6.0). After doing this and identifying a reengineering opportunity, the project team establishes the scope of the process-mapping project (Step 7.0). The next point, the mapping of the process (Step 8.0) starts. The project team maps the process using two methods, examines the constraints of the process, and finishes with a look at the people issues that affect the specific process. With all the prior information collected, the project team then designs a new process (Step 9.0), pilots the new process (Step 10.0), and if successful, applies the new process to the balance of the organization (Step 11.0).

STEP 6.0   IDENTIFY CURRENT BUSINESS PROCESSES.

In this step, the RSC identifies the few vital processes through which the organization meets its customers' needs regularly (see Figure 9.2). These critical processes respond to the needs of both internal

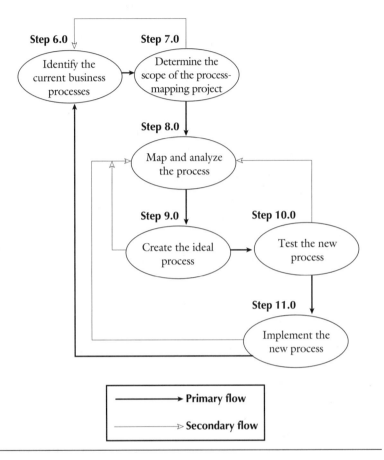

Figure 9.1. Phase III reengineering steps—designing change.

and external customers. They tend to be stable over time, and they should be directly linked to the organization's core competencies. Most important, this effort identifies the processes that can track and measure how well the organization is meeting its customers' needs.

Step 6.1   Determine the critical organizational processes.
With knowledge of the internal and external customers and their needs (Phase I), and of strategic and operational plans (Phase II), the RSC begins to identify the critical processes within the organization.

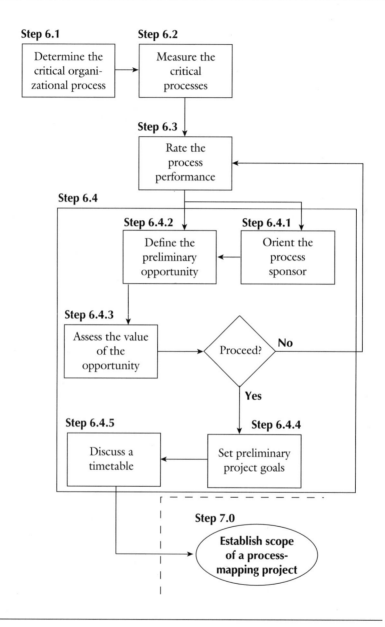

Figure 9.2. Step 6.0. Identify current business processes.

In total, the committee identifies six to 10 macroprocesses (for example, shipping and receiving, a specific product process, or data entry). These should be processes that are performed repeatedly, help fulfill the organization's mission, and help fulfill customer needs.

Example
At MTU—the example from chapter 1—an RSC was established and led by Gordon Weiner himself. After reviewing its operations, the RSC identified three critical processes: production of the MouseTrapper, scheduling, and factory control.

Step 6.2   Measure the critical processes.
Once critical processes have been identified, the RSC and line management must identify a method for tracking performance of each critical process. While an organization might begin by measuring only one critical process, over time a measure for all critical processes should be developed.

Once team members agree on a measure, they identify an existing data source or create a new data source to track this measure. The data generated are tracked and graphed for visual review of the ongoing process and progress.

Example
The MTU committee members decided to start with the production process. They choose this process because they felt it was the most critical to the company's operation. MTU's main production process consists of molding the various components, painting them assembling them as the MouseTrapper, and then packing and shipping them. Thus, the RSC started to collect molding, painting, and assembly data to measure the process.

Step 6.3   Rate the process performance.
Many methods can be used to rate or evaluate the performance of a process and determine whether an opportunity exists to improve its effectiveness, efficiency, and adaptability. However, two rating systems will be discussed here: benchmarking and process evaluation.

Benchmarking

Benchmarking studies can take many forms: telephone surveys, written questionnaires, literature searches, exchange of prepared materials, or site visits.[1] Benchmarking studies generally follow a four-step process: planning, collecting data, analyzing the data for performance gaps, and improving the process.

A benchmarking study can provide several outputs. First, it can compare performance of the benchmarked process among the target organizations. Second, it can describe an organization's gap in performance as compared to these identified performance levels. Third, it can identify best practices that produced the results observed during the study. Finally, the study can set performance goals for the process and identify areas where the sponsoring organization can improve performance.

Process evaluation

This tool, also used to evaluate a process for improvement opportunities, is the rating method develop by IBM.[2] The system is based on a five-level rating approach (see Figure 9.3).

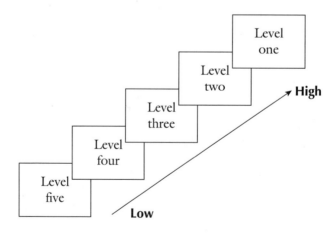

Figure 9.3. IBM's process rating system.

Processes at the lowest level, level five, have no designated owner. Moreover, process management is nonexistent, and the process itself may be ineffective. In addition, major deficiencies may exist that require corrective action.

At the next level up, level four, the basics of process management are in place, certain improvements have been identified, and corrective action plans have been established. To achieve this level, the following criteria must be met.

- A process owner must be identified and designated.
- Customer-supplier relationships and requirements, both internal and external to the process, must be established.
- The process must be defined and documented.
- Control points within the process must be found.
- Measurements of effectiveness and efficiency must be identified and put in place.
- The process must be assessed, and deficiencies or exposures such as defects, rework, excess cost, redundancies, or supplier problems, must be identified.
- Statistical methods must be set up and data collection must be underway.
- A defect method must be in place, and a feedback mechanism must be established for continuous quality improvement.

At the middle level, level three, the following criteria must be accomplished.

- Process-effectiveness measures must show evidence that customer requirements are being met.
- No significant control exposures must exist.
- Improvements needed to achieve level two must be identified, and a plan must be set in place to achieve this next level.

At level two, major improvements in the process have occurred, and positive results have been realized in terms of both efficiency and effectiveness. The process is also flexible enough to adapt to future demands that may be placed upon it. To achieve a level-two status, all elements comprising levels three and four must be in place. In addition, the following criteria must be met:

- Efficiency measures must show continuing reduction in resources per unit of work.
- The process must be competitive both in terms of effectiveness and efficiency as compared with comparable processes within the organization or industry.
- The process must be adaptable to business-direction changes without loss of efficiency and must be deemed by the customer to be able to meet requirements for several years.

Level one is the highest level obtainable. Here, the business process identified operates at maximum efficiency. It has been benchmarked or is considered a leader in this type of operation, and it functions at maximum effectiveness and adaptability. To achieve this rating, level-two and level-three requirements must be fulfilled in addition to the following criteria:

- The output must be primarily defect free.
- The process must operate with minimum resources.
- The process must be considered *best of class*—that is, it can be used as a model for benchmarking.

Example
At MTU, the committee examined all three processes and rated them using the process evaluation system. Here are its ratings for the three critical processes:

- Production—Level four
- Factory Control—Level four
- Scheduling—Level four

Thus, MTU's processes all need some major reengineering to bring them to top efficiency, effectiveness, and adaptability.

Step 6.4 Identifying opportunities and the process(es) to be reengineered.

Now that the various business processes have been identified, it is critical to decide whether any actually provide a reengineering opportunity. An opportunity may be lacking for several reasons:

- An inability to agree on the customer(s) of the process
- A lack of involvement by the process sponsor[3]
- Multiple potential process sponsors
- Unreasonable timing expectations
- Unresolved reengineering project questions and concerns
- An abundance of defensiveness and resistance to change

If any of these obstacles exists, your reengineering effort will be headed for failure. However, if an opportunity can be identified, the mapping project should further explore this opportunity.

6.4.1 Orient the process sponsor.

The process sponsor must be willing to make a commitment to the reengineering opportunity. If the process sponsor identifies the opportunity he or she also needs to explain the rationale for the reengineering effort. This will greatly help determine what goals the sponsor believes are most critical to the project's success. In addition, the sponsor should define the perceived problem and what effect he or she feels the reengineering effort will have on customer satisfaction. This orientation will build ownership in the design effort and increase the success and durability of any process improvement.

6.4.2 Define the preliminary opportunity.

Next, the process sponsor and the project leader must agree on

- Who are the process customers? Is there a primary customer, or do several customers have equal stake in the process?

- What is the process output in terms of products and/or services? What type(s) of transformation (physical, location, or transactional) occur within the process?

- How is customer satisfaction being measured? What is the current level of customer satisfaction with the process output? Do the customers have any particular concerns, such as quality or price?

- Are there any performance data that can help in evaluating the process's current performance?

- What are the perceived constraints of the process?

- How does this process compare with similar processes in other organizations—either internal or external?

If a reengineering opportunity exists, it will be identified by this information.

6.4.3 Assess the value of the opportunity.

Once the organization decides that a reengineering opportunity exists, the RSC must also decide whether the benefits outweigh the costs to change. That is, will the increases in efficiency, effectiveness, and adaptability exceed the cost of the resources the reengineering effort will consume? The value of the opportunity can be assessed by asking the four following questions:

1. Who would benefit most from improving this process?

2. Which individuals have an interest in the performance of the process?

3. Would these individuals recognize the value and priority of the effort?

4. Would improvements of the process improve the competitiveness (in terms of increased market share, throughput, quality, or profitability) of the organization?

Obviously, question four has the most importance in determining whether the reengineering effort should be undertaken. If a significant benefit would not be realized from the reengineering effort, the process should not be reengineered at this time. Typically, many significant reengineering opportunities exist within an organization and they are worth the time, effort, and resources that reengineering will consume. However, a single exception to this assertion exists. An organization may decide to reengineer a process as a learning experience, even if the specific reengineering opportunity will not reap a significant benefit. Applying the reengineering method to a small, minimally threatening process provides an excellent experience for a project team. Further, learning opportunities build the skills of team members and increase their commitment to, and acceptance of, a methodology for change before they tackle a major process reengineering effort.

6.4.4 Set preliminary project goals.
Once an opportunity is identified and its value assessed, the next step is to establish preliminary project goals, such as an increase in quality or a reduction in cycle time. Next, the project leader should ask whether these goals can be realized. The final question is whether the preliminary project goals provide enough challenge and excitement so that members of the organization will want to attain them. In other words, will the organization buy into the project?

6.4.5 Discuss a timetable.
The final task is to allow reasonable time for achieving the goals. For example, if the opportunity identified involves a complete redesign of the organization's production-management system, and the vice president of operations wants the process team to complete the project within four weeks, a serious conflict may result. The process team must set a reasonable timetable to achieve its goals. Further, management must give the team the time necessary to accomplish more than a quick fix of the process.

STEP 7.0 ESTABLISH THE SCOPE OF THE PROCESS-MAPPING PROJECT.

The project leader establishes the scope of the project by identifying the process stakeholders, creating a project mission and goals, structuring and selecting team members, and finally, developing a work plan to carry out the project (see Figure 9.4).

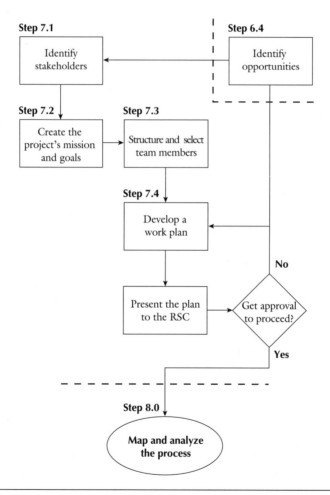

Figure 9.4. Step 7.0. Establish the scope of the project.

Step 7.1   Identify process stakeholders.

In this substep, the leader of the mapping project works with the process sponsor(s) to identify the process stakeholders. A *stakeholder* is anyone who has an interest in the process being explored: the employees who perform the tasks of the process, the organization as a whole, or even the community that has an interest in seeing the process operate to keep community members employed. However, in this substep, it is important to identify those stakeholders who have a primary or direct interest in the process being explored. The project leader and process sponsor should look internally to the organization and ask, "Which individuals can best represent these organizations (based on who is affected by the process), and who has the authority to make changes?"

After the process stakeholders have been identified, the project leader must confirm that the sponsor(s) will take the lead role in gaining commitment from stakeholders. First, this establishes that the process sponsor will actively participate in the reengineering process. Second, commitment from stakeholders is necessary—even those stakeholders directly involved with the reengineering process. Further, gaining commitment orients stakeholders both to the process reengineering and to the specifics of the forthcoming activity.

Once all the process stakeholders have been identified and oriented to the upcoming activity, the project leader proceeds to the next substep, establishing the project's mission and goals.

Step 7.2   Create the project's mission and goals.

The project leader's first activity is to clarify his or her assumptions about the project. Specifically, the project leader must identify any assumptions or constraints that will affect the change that can be made to the process. Examples of such assumptions include the following:

- Expected level of improvement
- Resources (time, cost, or personnel constraints)
- Areas or issues that are off-limits

- Potential changes in other processes that may affect this process
- Potential organizational conflicts

Next, a project leader must establish the preliminary boundaries of the project. That is, the leader should select the primary customer and products or services outputs of the process. He or she also needs to identify the initial inputs to the process. Inputs include the people, materials, equipment, and general working environment involved in the process. After identifying the initial inputs and the process outputs, the project leader will know the general boundaries of the process to be reengineered.

Additionally, the project leader must ask, "What organization(s) is (are) included within the boundaries?" The answer to this question may identify several additional customers the project leader and sponsor had not considered. Finally, the leader must ask whether there are any potential problems or challenges (for example, political, too broad in scope, etc.) in using these boundaries. If the answer is yes, the project leader must reconsider the scope of the project.

After identifying as many potential obstacles as possible, the project leader must develop a preliminary project mission statement and preliminary project goals, and then send them to the stakeholders for review. The stakeholders must concur with the identified opportunity, the goals, the boundaries, and the assumptions. Without this concurrence, any reengineering effort will fail. If the stakeholders will not agree with the project goals and methods, the project needs to be delayed, or appropriate changes to the project must be made to gain the concurrence of the stakeholders. If appropriate changes are made and stakeholders still do not concur, other reengineering opportunities should be explored.

Step 7.3   Structure and select team members.

After the project mission statement and goals are created, the project leader, with assistance from the sponsor and the stakeholders (if possible), must identify the individuals who should be members of this reengineering project. The following questions may help in identifying the individuals who should be on the project team.

- Which individuals have the greatest knowledge of, experience with, and influence over portions of the process?

- Who must be contacted to ensure these people are available for the effort?

- Who might serve as alternatives if they are unavailable?

Once the team members are selected, the project leader should call a meeting to inform the members of the ground rules of the project and present the project's mission and goals. The project leader should ensure that all team members buy into the project's missions and goals by soliciting their input and revising the project's missions and goals as necessary. The project leader should also provide the team with the preliminary decisions (for example, budget constraints, and so on) made by the sponsor(s) and the stakeholders. After the orientation meeting, the project leader should identify and resolve any issues or concerns brought up by the team.

Step 7.4   Develop a work plan.

As a group, the team must complete the project's mission and goals. Initially, the team as a whole should develop a work plan that covers the following points:

1. The tasks to be performed during the mapping effort (Step 8.0)
2. The individuals responsible for those tasks
3. An estimate of the timing for completion of the tasks

The next activity is to determine the frequency of meetings, the length of the process, the requirements of team members, and a schedule for periodic review of the work plan by stakeholders. The final activity is to present the work plan to the RSC for approval. This presentation should clarify whether the sponsor, the stakeholders, and the leader agree on the following:

1. Project assumptions

2. Project goals

3. Clarity of tasks and assignments

4. Division of work

Notes

1. An excellent source for benchmarking information is *Planning, Organizing, and Managing Benchmarking Activities: A User's Guide*, offered by the International Benchmark Clearinghouse, 123 North Post Oak Lane, Suite 300, Houston, TX 77024-7797; 800-366-9606.

2. Kane, E. J. "IBM's Quality Focus on the Business Process," *Quality Progress* (April 1986): 24.

3. A *process sponsor* is the individual who either owns the process or is responsible for the successful operation of that process. Typically, the process sponsor is the liaison between the reengineering team and the process stakeholders.

CHAPTER 10

Reengineering Steps
Part 2

A t this point, all preliminary steps have been completed (process identification and scope definition). In addition, a reengineering project has been identified and a work plan has been established. Now the reengineering team starts mapping and analyzing the process.

STEP 8.0   MAP AND ANALYZE THE PROCESS.

In this step of the reengineering model, the project team will map the process to be reengineered twice. First, the team will map the process using a standard industrial engineering method—a flowchart. A flowchart shows the logical progression of tasks and control points. However, a flowchart contains a very limited view of the process being examined. Second, to help overcome these limitations, the team will map the process using an integrated flow diagram (IFD). An IFD maps the communication patterns of the process being reviewed. Typically, an IFD and flowchart reveal very different views of the process.

When both maps are available, the reengineering team will examine the constraints of the existing process by performing a process-constraint analysis and a cultural-factor analysis of the process (see Figure 10.1).

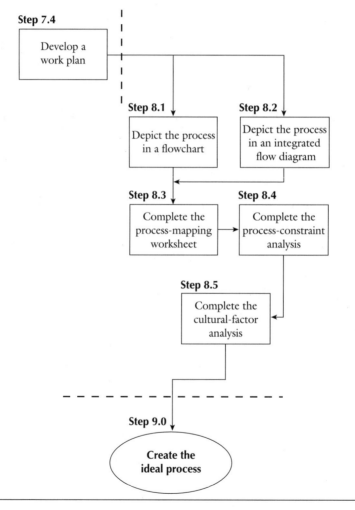

Figure 10.1. Step 8.0. Map and analyze the process.

Step 8.1   Depict the process in a flowchart.

Flowcharts graphically describe the sequence of activities in a process. A graphic description, such as a flowchart, is generally more useful than a written description of a process, because most people are visually oriented.

Five basic methods may be used to chart a process. Each has its own standard set of symbols. The first method is used by leading accounting firms. In this method, the rectangle identifies a processor document. A large diamond identifies a decision point. Typically, a decision refers to some type of control activity, such as the decision to proceed or to stop the processes. Arrows show the direction of work flow. Other symbols include small squares and diamonds. The two symbols represent check and compare points respectively (see Figure 10.2).

The symbols in the second method conform to the DIN (Deutsches Institut für Normung e.V) information-processing standard. They are similar to the shapes used for the International Standard ISO 5807 of the International Organization for Standardization (see Figure 10.3).

The third method uses shapes found in various quality management programs, including those that support ISO 9000, a set of international standards for a quality assurance management system (see Figure 10.4).

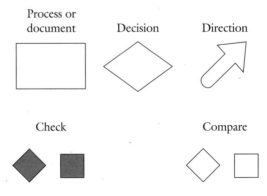

Figure 10.2. Auditing flowchart symbols.

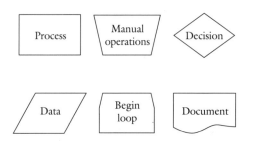

Figure 10.3. DIN flowchart symbols.

The fourth set of flowchart symbols are typically used for operations engineering (OE) and in process quality management and improvement flowcharts.[1] These symbols are used by many telephone companies (see Figure 10.5).

The final group of symbols are those used for standard information flowcharts.[2] Figure 10.6 illustrates these symbols.

No matter which flowchart symbols are used, however, flowcharting should be conducted on two or three levels. Level-1 flowcharts define the key activities in the process at the macrolevel. A level-1 flowchart comprises several groups of activities and reflects the principle transformations that occur between groupings. Typically, several activities are contained within a single rectangle.

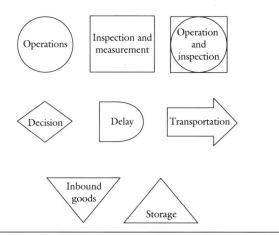

Figure 10.4. ISO 9000 flowchart symbols.

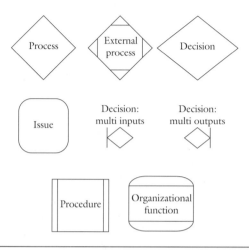

Figure 10.5. Flowchart symbols from OE and process quality management and improvement.

Level-2 flowcharts, depicting the next level of detail, display activities using the level-1 chart as a guide. At this point, however, the team must distinguish between an activity and a task. A *task* is the most basic unit in the process hierarchy, while an *activity* consists of several tasks linked together. A level-2 flowchart displays the process with moderate detail. However, a level-2 flowchart does not contain too much detail compared with a level-1 flowchart, which does not contain sufficient detail to identify process-enhancement opportunities. However, a very detailed flowchart (level 3) identifying tasks rather than activities can provide too much detail and cause confusion. Too much detail can also convey such an overwhelming amount of information that the team has problems identifying a starting point for the analysis.

Occasionally, a level-3 flowchart is necessary when a level-2 flowchart does not lend itself to analysis. A level-3 flowchart displays the process at the task level only. However, a level-2 flowchart is usually sufficient to identify specific reengineering opportunities. Further, once the level-2 (activity) flowchart is complete, specific activities can be mapped at the task level if necessary.

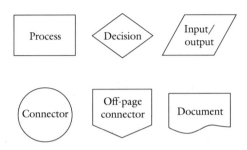

Figure 10.6. Standard information flowchart symbols.

The first step in flowcharting is to identify the boundaries. Starting with the input boundary, the team identifies the corresponding outputs and draws them on the chart with appropriate labeling. The rest of the chart should depict the work flow through successive transformation and control steps from input to outputs. Thus, the team keeps asking, "What is the next activity that is performed?" Specific activities with corresponding inputs and outputs are then added to the chart using the appropriate symbols and labels. These steps are repeated until the last activity is drawn and labeled.

The team can identify the inputs and the outputs by asking the following questions.

- What work product, information, or materials are needed as inputs to this activity?
- What are the requirements of these inputs?
- Does an interface exist between this activity and the preceding one?
- Does the activity involve a decision that leads to either of two output states?

A flowchart can be drawn either horizontally or vertically depending on the team's preference or the readability of the chart. If the flowchart is drawn horizontally, boundary lines should be drawn to the left of the first activity symbol and to the right of the last activity symbol (assuming a left-to-right activity flow). Similarly, if the process is depicted vertically, boundary lines should be drawn above the first activity symbol and below the last activity symbol (assuming a top-to-bottom activity flow).

The flowchart should also depict departmental borders. This simple step allows the project team to focus on the output requirements as seen by the recipient (customer) of the work product—the department or party next in line in the flow of work. Many problems occurring in administrative-service processes result from the lack of communication between the process and recipient.

Example
At MTU, the reengineering team produced a flowchart of the main production process. The level-1 flowchart the team created is displayed in Figure 10.7.

Review the completed flowchart.
After the flowcharts are complete, the team members must review them. If team members disagree over the accuracy of flowcharts, the project leader must find and resolve the reasons for conflicting views. Also, the team must ensure that additional information (a level-3 flowchart) is not required to gain a better understanding of the process. Once agreement is reached, the project team can proceed with an IFD.

Notes
1. More information on these symbols can be found in *Operations Engineering Workbook: An Action Oriented Approach to Implement PQMI* (Holmdel, N.J.: AT&T Bell Laboratories, 1992).

2. Most are based on an appendix to the document "American National Standard for Information and Image Mangagement— Flowcharting Symbol and Their Use in Micrographics, ANSI/AIIM MS4-1987." More information on these symbols can be found in ANSI X3.5-1970 and 5807-1985(E), "Information Processing—Document Symbols and Conventions for Data, Program and System Flowcharts, Program Network Charts and System Resource Charts." For futher information, contact American National Standards Institute, 11 West 42nd Street, New York, NY 10036.

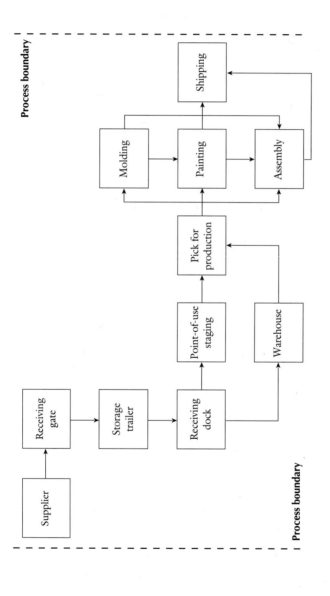

Figure 10.7. Level–1 production flowchart of Mouse Traps Unlimited.

CHAPTER 11

Reengineering Steps Part 3

Step 8.2   Depict the process in an integrated flow diagram.

An IFD is a graphic representation of the physical and communication patterns of a process. An IFD is made up of four basic elements.

1. Pipelines
2. Activities
3. Files
4. External entities

A simple example of an IFD appears in Figure 11.1.

In this example, X arrive from the external entity S and are transformed into two parts, A and B by activity P_1. A and B are

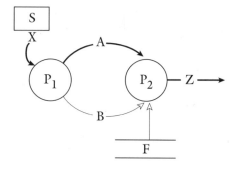

Figure 11.1. Elements of an IFD.

subsequently transformed into Zs by the process P_2, which requires C from file F as an additional input.

The symbols and method used to complete an IFD are adapted from the system-analysis technique called *data flow diagraming*. There are two styles for depicting data flow: the Yourdon-DeMarco style and the Gane & Sarson style.[1] Figure 11.2 displays the symbols used by each. The principle differences between the IFD and the data flow diagram involve their application and scope. For example, data flow diagrams were designed for data processing applications, whereas the IFD can be used for any business process. Further, both data flow diagrams and IFDs show information flows, but in addition, IFDs show the flow of physical products through the process. More detail regarding IFD components appears in the sections that follow.

Pipelines

A pipeline moves a single *package* of information or material between the activities, files, and external entities on an IFD. A pipeline is symbolized by a named vector or arrow to show the interface. For example, Mouse Traps Unlimited identified a pipeline called *molded material*. Further, it defined molded material as a molded piece of plastic and a production slip. In this example, both the molded piece and the production slip make up a single package of information, meaning that the next operation needs both pieces

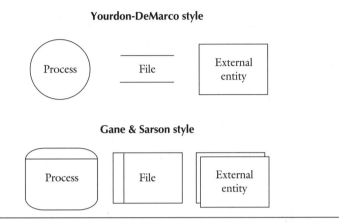

Figure 11.2. Data flow styles.

together. In addition, because the primary item in this package is the material, the pipeline is represented with a thick line (see Figure 11.3).

In the next example, two separate pipelines move between two activities. The information in the pipelines is independent of each other. Thus, it never travels together. Here, the molded material (which consists of the plastic item and production slip) travels from molding to assembly. The second pipeline sends the part status, a report. Because this pipeline is sending only information, it is represented by a thin line and arrow (see Figure 11.4). A useful set of conventions exists for dealing with pipelines.

- No two pipelines have the same name.
- Names are chosen to represent not only the package that moves over the pipeline, but also what is known about the package.
- Pipelines that move into and out of files do not require names; the file name will suffice to describe the pipeline. All other pipelines must be named.
- Thin lines, thick lines, and broken lines can be used to distinguish between types of pipelines.

Figure 11.3. Material pipeline in an IFD.

The thick-line vector often represents a flow of physical materials from process to process, such as the movement of tape from a storage facility to a tape silo. In turn, a thin-line vector represents the flow of information, such as reports or telephone calls between activities. However, some IFD creators use the thick line to show the principal flow, or main manufacturing pipelines, while using thin lines to represent support pipelines, like scheduling and production control. The purpose of the IFD is to represent the flow of all physical items and communication patterns within the process. The IFD's creator, however, may apply a variety of individual conventions.

Here are some additional notes regarding IFDs and pipelines: First, control points are not represented on an IFD. Such items are represented on a flowchart, not an IFD. Second, if a pipeline

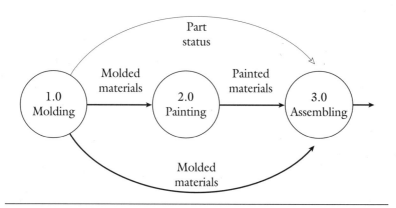

Figure 11.4. Material and information pipelines in an IFD.

cannot easily be named, the pipeline is probably not defined adequately. Either several packages are being transmitted along the pipeline, or an incomplete package is being transmitted.

Activities

Activities invariably represent some amount of work performed on the package from the pipeline. A common convention is to represent activities by circles (bubbles) on the IFD. However, an activity can also be represented by an oval. Whatever its shape, each activity needs a descriptive name. Further, if the name does not clearly describe the activity, the IFD will not convey the big picture to the IFD's reviewer.

Finally, in completed sets of IFDs, each activity will be numbered. The numbering convention will depend on how the various diagrams interrelate.

Files

A *file* is a collection of information or material, or a space where this information or material is stored. For an IFD, a file is any temporary repository for the information or material. A *file* may be a computer tape, a specific area on a computer disk, a card data set, an index file, or an address book. A file might also be a wastebasket (a circular file). Any temporary repository qualifies as a file. A file is often represented by a double straight line with the file's name in close proximity. Finally, an IFD should be meaningful to its individual users, so file names must also be meaningful. In other words, avoid using coded names for files. Moreover, no two files should have the same name on a single IFD.

External Entities

Any process can be described on an IFD with pipelines, activities, and files. However, an IFD is clarified by being shown in the larger context of external entities. An *external entity* can be defined as a person or organization outside the boundary of the process that is a net originator or receiver of the process being mapped. The key qualifier here is *outside the boundary of the process.* A person or organization *inside* the boundaries of the process is characterized by an activity on the IFD.

By convention, external entities are represented by named boxes. Pipelines may flow into and out of a single box. Boxes, however, should be used sparingly in the IFD, and they should not represent major concerns. External entity boxes exist only to provide commentary about the process's connection to the outside world. If a box represents a major concern in an IFD, the boundaries of the process are probably not defined correctly.

Guidelines for Drawing IFDs

When attempting to draw an IFD for a particular process, the following five steps are recommended.

1. Identify net input and output pipelines. Draw the input and output pipelines around the outside of the diagram.
2. Identify the internal pipelines and activities by examining the actual work practices of the process. Fill in the body of the IFD with the internal pipeline.
3. Label the pipelines.
4. Label the activities.
5. Be prepared to start over.

In the following sections, each of these five steps will be presented in greater detail.

8.2.1 Identify net input and output pipelines.

The business of deciding net inputs and outputs is closely tied to the decision about the boundaries of the reengineering project. Selecting the initial boundary is a matter of judgment and feel. The reengineering team must select a boundary that is large enough to include all activities relevant to the reengineering effort, but small enough to exclude irrelevant activities.

After defining the boundaries of the project, examine the pipelines that cross those boundaries. These pipelines are the *net inputs and outputs*. List the net inputs and outputs on the periphery of the diagram.

Two notes: first, use a broken line to define net input and output pipelines so the boundaries can be identified with a quick glance (see Figure 11.5). Second, don't be too worried about being thorough at this point. The process of developing an IFD includes self-checking mechanisms that identify forgotten pipelines.

8.2.2 *Fill in the body of the IFD*

First, concentrate on pipelines—in particular, any major pipelines moving about the process. For example, in the production process at MTU the major pipeline is the flow of material through the production process. Thus, the reengineering team would enter that major pipeline on the diagram and connect it with the pipelines on the periphery. Place bubbles wherever work is required to transform one package into another package. Don't name these activities—leave them blank—they will be named later (see Figure 11.6).

Now, examine the activities that have been identified on the IFD. Are any of these activities connected with pipelines? Identify any internal pipelines that may be used within activities. Discuss these internal pipelines with individuals inside the process to decide if any single activity should be replaced with two (or three or four) activities. If so, mark all pipelines between these added activities (see Figure 11.7).

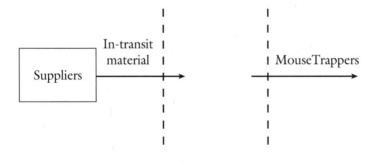

Figure 11.5. Identify net pipelines.

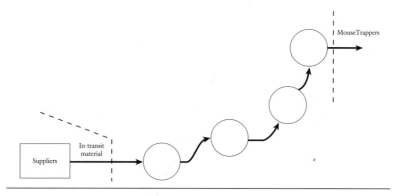

Figure 11.6. Filling in the body of the IFD: Part 1.

For each activity, the reengineering team should ask the following questions:

- What components (packages from other pipelines) or activities, if any, are needed to transform this item?
- Where do the components come from?

While filling in activities and pipelines, also enter files on the IFD to represent any repositories that the user discusses.

If necessary, modify the boundary of the process being mapped. An unidentified input may be a key component of one of the pipelines. Further, if an incoming pipeline could be eliminated and have no effect on the process, remove it. You may discover that the process includes not one but two disconnected networks—one of which is outside the domain of the study. In such a case, eliminate the network that is not being studied from the diagram.

8.2.3 Label the pipelines.
The names selected for pipelines greatly affect the clarity of the IFD (see Figure 11.8). The following are suggestions for naming pipelines:

- Avoid generic names such as *data* and *information*.
- No two pipelines should have the same name.

- Names should represent not only the package that moves through the pipeline, but also what is known about the package.
- Pipelines that move into and out of files do not require names; the file name will suffice to describe the pipeline. All other pipelines must be named.

8.2.4 Label the activities.

After the pipelines are labeled, label the activities (see Figure 11.9). Below are some suggestions for naming activities:

- Make sure the activity names honestly reflect the activity. For example, *painting* is not an appropriate name if the activity paints a part, drills holes in the part, and inserts a second part into the drilled holes.
- Activity names should consist of a single strong action verb and a single object. If there are two verbs, further partitioning should be considered.
- Partition a difficult-to-name process into two or three activities, or group several activities to identify a process that can be more easily named.

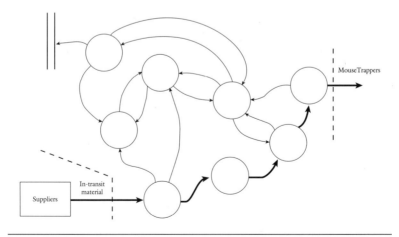

Figure 11.7. Filling in the body of the IFD: Part 2.

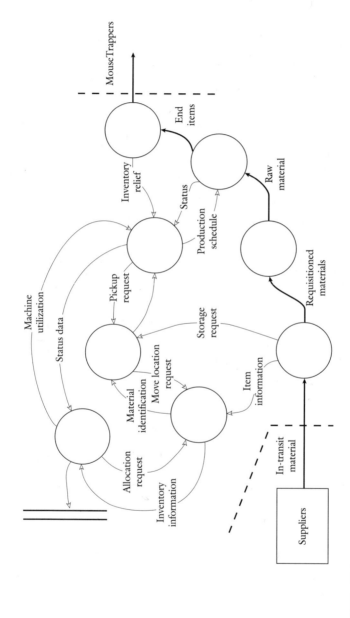

Figure 11.8. Fill in the pipelines.

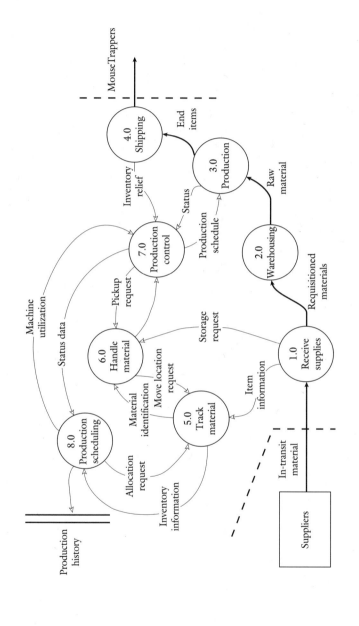

Figure 11.9. Label the activities.

START OVER

Mapping a process with an IFD is not easy, and a reengineering team will rarely map the process correctly the first time. False starts and iterations will be needed to produce an appropriate IFD approach. Typically, however, a team's subsequent IFDs are vastly improved over earlier versions, which should be considered learning experiences. The reengineering team should start over any time it feels that significantly better results can be accomplished.

Note
1. DeMarco, Tom. *Structured Analysis and System Specification.* (New York: Yourdon, Inc., 1979).

Reengineering Steps Part 4

Step 8.3   Complete the process-mapping worksheet.

After completing the required flowchart(s) and IFD(s) of the process, the reengineering team should complete the process-mapping worksheet (see Figures 12.1 and 12.2). This worksheet provides an executive summary of the process in a consolidated format. Typically, the many pages of flowcharts and IFDs tend to overwhelm the process sponsor, stakeholders, and RSC members—especially if these individuals have not been involved in the daily activity of the reengineering project. Thus, the team should complete the following items in sequential order, using all the material collected up to this point.

Process-Mapping Worksheet

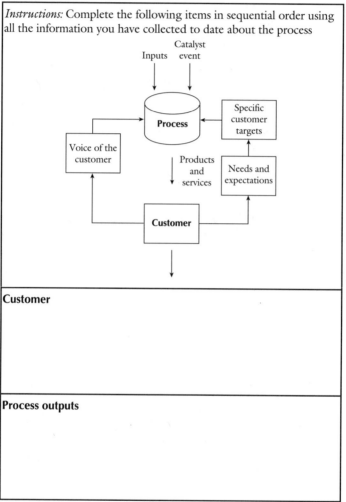

Figure 12.1. Process-mapping worksheet.

Customer section

Customers are the users of the products or services produced by the process. Customers are the ultimate judges of the quality of the

Process inputs
Catalyst event
Customer needs and expectations
Specific customer targets
Voice of the customer
Specific process targets
Voice of the process

Figure 12.2. Process-mapping worksheet (continued).

process outputs. Furthermore, the primary customer is the most important customer for the specific product or service—the principal reason the process exists and the end boundary of the process. The primary customer should be identified here.

Process outputs section

The *process outputs* are the products or services produced by the process. The reengineering team should list the products and services produced by the process here.

Process inputs section

Process inputs are the equipment, materials, methods, and environment necessary to produce the products and services of the process. People are the central resources who take the inputs and act upon them. The information for this section can be obtained directly from the flowcharts and IFDs.

Catalyst event section

The *catalyst event* is the event that signals the beginning of the process. The catalyst establishes the initial boundary of the process. The catalyst event can be found on the first-level drawing of the IFD or the level-1 flowchart.

Customer needs and expectations section

This section illustrates the attributes of the products and services that customers require. The material for this section can be found on either of the mapping pictures. If the team cannot identify the customers' needs and expectations in one of the mapping pictures, the information can be obtained from the process sponsor or stakeholders.

Specific customer targets section

Specific customer targets translate customers' needs and expectations into specific, quantifiable attributes that can be used to assess the quality of the product or service.

Voice of the customer section

The *voice of the customer* is the feedback mechanism by which the customers' satisfaction with the product or service is measured and examined. To properly identify and understand the voice of the customers, the team must answer the following three questions.

1. How well does the process satisfy your customer(s)?

2. How do you find out whether you are meeting the needs and expectations of your customer(s)?

3. Do the measures being used assess the voice of your customer(s)?

Specific process targets section

This section defines the objectives, goals, and targets that the process must achieve to meet product or service quality expectations of the customers. These targets are a direct translation of the specific customer targets.

Voice of the process section

The *voice of the process* is the feedback mechanism by which the quality of the process is measured and examined against the specific process targets. This measurement and examination is done before the product or service gets to the customer. To properly identify and understand the voice of the process, the team should ask the following seven questions.

1. What critical characteristics of the process can be improved so that the products and services will meet or exceed the customers' needs and expectations?

2. What targets (improvements) should be established so that the critical characteristics will meet or exceed the customers' needs and expectations?

3. What additional information is needed to define these targets?

4. What should be measured inside or during the process?

5. Is there a system for collecting information on the performance of the process?

6. Do the measurements being used to assess the voice of the process reflect the voice of the customers?

7. Is the process currently meeting the established targets for the critical characteristics of the process?

Step 8.4   Complete the process-constraint analysis.

A *process-constraint analysis* is a brief examination of those obstacles that prevent the process from satisfying the customer or from operating effectively and efficiently. The process-constraint analysis worksheet can be used to organize the findings (see Figure 12.3). To begin the analysis, the team must identify the obstacles that prevent the employees who are part of the process from doing their work properly. The best source for this information is the employees themselves. Simply ask them what is preventing them from doing their job. After listening to the answers, the team needs to identify where, and why, the constraints are occurring.

The reengineering team must decide if a particular constraint is a *true constraint* or a *self-imposed constraint*. A *true constraint* is one that is hard to overcome or needs capital improvements to overcome. Examples include the size of a room or building, the capacity of a particular machine, the need for a piece of equipment, or law or regulation that requires an organization to perform (or not perform) certain types of activities. In contrast, a *self-imposed constraint* is a constraint that the organization imposes upon itself and that can be removed. Examples include employee dress codes, approval signatures, and internal rules and policies. Organizational structure or functional/departmental structure may also represent self-imposed constraints.

The reengineering team cannot overcome a process constraint without knowing where and why it exists. However, once the team identifies why the constraint exists and where in the process it is located, members can start on the path to removing the constraint.

Step 8.5 Complete the cultural factor analysis.
All activities involve people. If the individuals involved with the process feel that they have little or no control over their work environment, the process faces the possibility of failure. However, too much control can also lead to process failure. Feelings of control or lack of control spring from the culture of an organization. Thus, the team needs to rate the cultural factors associated with a particular process. When this analysis is completed, the reengineered process should be corrected. Without a cultural-factor analysis, the reengineering team may reengineer a process and reduce positive cultural factors, which could increase the possibility of process failure.

In the 1950s, Fred Emery and Eric Trist defined six factors common to all studies of culture and employee motivation. These factors, set in a two-level framework, directly correlate with commitment, high productivity, and lower absenteeism and turnover.

Process-constraint analysis

Constraints	Where did it occur?	Why did it happen?	The impact or result of the constraint
1			
2			
3			
4			

Figure 12.3. Process-constraint analysis worksheet.

Level 1—Optimum factors

According to Emery and Trist, the first three factors—empowerment, variety of task, and feedback/learning—occur at a specific optimum level in organizations (that is, a process may have too much or too little of that particular factor).

1. *Empowerment.* Empowerment is the ability of the individual to make a decision that affects the work environment. This includes controlling time, schedule, materials, and work pace. If an employee has too little empowerment, he or she feels controlled or imposed upon. However, if employees have too much empowerment, the result is chaos and confusion. For example, without realizing the impact, employees with too much empowerment may make wide-sweeping decisions that affect other departments or organizations. Thus, employees should be empowered, but an employee's empowerment should have limits.

2. *Variety of task.* Variety of task involves the issue of specialization. As stated earlier, the path of specialization has led many American businesses to the trouble they are currently experiencing. Businesses have reduced each activity to small, redundant tasks (the

foundation of traditional manufacturing). And this lack of variety leads to an increase of boredom and lack of job motivation, which in turn, increases errors.

However, too much variety can lead to employee paralysis. An employee may have so much variety that he or she ends up confused and does nothing at all. Thus, each employee should have sufficient variety of tasks to promote interest. However, a limit on this variety is needed to eliminate anxiety and confusion

3. *Feedback/learning.* The feedback/learning factor concerns both the timeliness and the amount of data regarding goals achievement that an employee receives from management. Too much feedback and close supervision (standing over an employee's shoulder) cause overload and low moral. Too little feedback, however, allows an employee to fail. Enough feedback should be given to promote self-control and learning. Further, feedback should be built into the task wherever possible.

Level 2— Maximal factors

Organizations can have too little of the next three factors, but not too much.

1. *Mutual support/respect.* Mutual support and respect among employees are critical for process success. At the maximum level, employees feel few or no perceived barriers regarding levels, status, and opportunities. They feel valued. With little or no mutual support and respect, employees feel subservient or looked down upon. In this case, both morale and employee performance suffer.

2. *Big picture.* Employees like to, and need to, know how their work contributes to the whole. In other words, employees need to see the big picture. Without the big picture, employees do not know the impact of their actions on the processes downstream from them. Further, they may not care.

3. *Career pathing.* All employees need to know that there is opportunity for growth—that the position they fill is not a dead-end job. Each employee must continue to learn and must be able to move to other jobs, departments, and divisions. If an employee feels a career path is not available, he or she may leave the organization or "internally retire." An employee who has internally retired does just enough work to get by and lacks both job motivation and job

satisfaction. An employee who has internally retired is an obstacle to success of the process.

Rate the cultural factors.

The reengineering team, using the cultural matrix shown in Figure 12.4, assesses the six cultural factors of the process. It does so by either interviewing or surveying the employees who are involved with the process and then rating each position within the process according to the following scales:

Optimum factors: − 5 to + 5, 0 = just right

Maximal factors: 0 to 10; 0 = none, 10 = a great deal.

Once all rating is completed, the reengineering team moves to the next step, creating the ideal process.

STEP 9.0   CREATE THE IDEAL PROCESS.

At this point, the project team has all the information it needs to create the ideal process. However, several issues should be addressed before the team creates the new process.

First, the team needs to assess the readiness of the organization to generate the ideal process and accept the proposed change. This assessment is accomplished by asking the following three questions.

1. Have all appropriate stakeholders, including customers, been involved in progress to date?

2. Do the team members fully understand the way the process works today, and is that understanding supported with quantitative and qualitative data?

3. Has the process been analyzed to a level of detail that allows alternative processes to be generated easily?

If the organization is ready to generate the ideal process, the team needs to decide the criteria that will demonstrate the success of the change. These criteria should reflect the customers' targets and the overall project goals. Also, the team needs to decide if any true constraints exist that will limit the process changes (see Figure 12.5).

Rating the cultural factors

In the space below, rate each of the cultural factors by using the following scale:

    Optimum factors: – 5 to + 5; 0 = just right.
    Maximal factors: 0 to 10; 0 = none, 10 = a great deal.

Optimum factors

Job title	Empowerment	Variety	Feedback

Maximal factors

Respect	Big picture	Growth

Figure 12.4. Cultural-factor analysis worksheet.

Step 9.1   Describe the ideal process on paper.

The reengineering team should put all its papers—flowcharts, IFDs, process-constraint matrixes, and cultural-factor analysis sheets—except the process-mapping worksheet out of sight. Then, using the information on the process-mapping worksheet and the team's knowledge of the process, the team creates the ideal process—a process with no constraints (self-imposed or true). The team should create a flowchart and an IFD of the ideal process on a flip chart or a chalkboard. When these diagrams are complete, the project leader should ask the following questions.

- Has the team tried to design the ideal process, ignoring present constraints?

- If not, what alternatives could be developed if underlying true constraints or assumptions about the process were removed?

- How could these constraints be removed or satisfied in a different way?

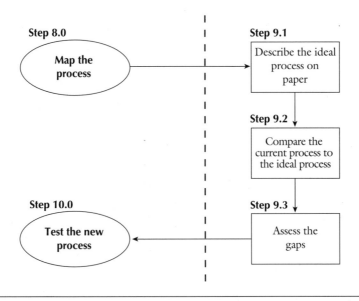

Figure 12.5. Step 9.0. Create the ideal process.

Step 9.2   Compare the current process to the ideal process.

The reengineering team then should compare its ideal process with the present process and look for the differences (gaps) between them.

Step 9.3   Assess the gaps.

The team needs to decide how the gaps between the present process and ideal process can be closed. Once alternatives (changes in the existing process) to close the gaps are identified, the team should consider the five following questions.

1. With the changes, will the process meet the goals of the project?
2. To what degree will the changes reduce the difference between the voice of the process and the voice of the customer?
3. Will the stakeholders agree to the changes, and will individuals in the process agree to the changes?
4. If not, what alternative action can the team take?
   - Which of the alternatives has the greatest likelihood of success in terms of application and impact?
   - Can the team estimate the extent to which improvement will close the gap between the present process and the ideal process?

STEP 10.0   TEST THE NEW PROCESS.

The project team is finally ready to apply its findings and improvements, at least in a small-scale demonstration or pilot project. Usually, however, the reengineering team does not have to carry out its findings carte blanche. First, the proposed changes must be presented to and approved by the RSC and the stakeholders.

Step 10.1   Develop pilot objective.

The team should clarify its pilot objectives and success factors before discussing its proposal the RSC and the stakeholders.

The objectives of the pilot process can be assessed by asking the following questions.

- What is the team trying to accomplish by running the pilot? The desired accomplishments need to be documented so the committee can make an informed decision.

- What factors are needed to create a realistic environment to run the pilot? Piloting a new process in a service organization is easier than piloting a new process in a manufacturing environment. In a manufacturing process, capital, new equipment, and extensive training may be required to pilot the new process.

- What factors or characteristics have to be present for the pilot?

Step 10.2   Develop pilot measures.

The measurements needed to determine the success of the pilot process can be assessed by asking the following questions.

- What indicators or factors are key in determining whether a change to the process has been successful?

- Which indicators will be measured, and how will they be measured?

- What tools can be used to measure the effects of the changes?

- Are the success indicators consistent with the process targets and the overall goals of the project?

- Is the customer of the process aware of the pilot project and its objectives?

Only after answering these questions and preparing a formal presentation should the project team present its findings to the

RSC and the process stakeholders for agreement and approval to proceed (see Figure 12.6).

Step 10.3 Gain agreement and approval from stakeholders.

At the formal presentation to the RSC and the stakeholders, the team will need to answer the following questions. First, where will the pilot take place, and what are the risks and benefits of conducting the pilot at this location? Next, which individuals will be

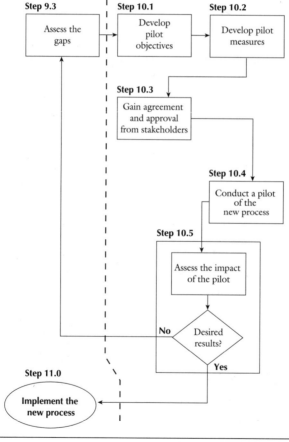

Figure 12.6. Step 10.0. Test the new process.

involved in the pilot? Individuals are needed both for changing the process and for measuring the results. Further, have the individuals who have not been involved to date in the reengineering project been oriented to the team's findings and the need to pilot the potential changes?

Step 10.4   Conduct a pilot of the new process.

Once the team has gained approval to proceed, it is important to clarify the following three points to all pilot participants.

1. The changes that are taking place and why they are happening
2. Where changes are taking place
3. What, if any, new skills or perspectives are needed by pilot participants

Clarifying these points with the pilot participants greatly increases the potential for success of the pilot by building commitment and buy-in. Further, pilot participants need the opportunity to state their concerns, and these concerns need to be addressed before proceeding with the pilot. Once all concerns are addressed, conduct the pilot.

Step 10.5   Assess the impact of the pilot.

After a predetermined period, the reengineering team needs to assess the impact of the pilot. Specifically, it must decide whether the data collected from the pilot support the conclusion that a real change occurred in process performance. That is, do the indicators show improvement to a level beyond normal statistical variations? More important, does the customer notice a difference in the product or service received? Does the change being measured reflect what the customer really wants?

After analyzing the data received from the pilot, the team must summarize the findings for another presentation to the RSC. Specifically, the team should address the following three questions.

1. How do the results of the pilot compare with what the team thought would happen?

2. Do all team members agree in their interpretation of the data? If not, why are there differences?

3. Are there any reasons why the lessons of the pilot should not be introduced to other parts of the organization?

STEP 11.0 IMPLEMENT THE NEW PROCESS.

During the presentation to the RSC, the reengineering team must make sure that all the stakeholders understand, concur with, and agree to support the findings of the pilot. Further, all must agree that the environment where the pilot was performed permits generalization of the results to the whole organization. If both conditions are met, the reengineering team and the RSC need to prepare for full application of the new process (see Figure 12.7). They do so by developing an implementation action plan.

Step 11.1 Develop an implementation action plan.

The implementation action plan needs to be comprehensive so that the transition from the old process to the new one flows smoothly and without major pain or trauma. As stated earlier in this book, change is a slow process. Humans typically avoid change. Thus, a comprehensive implementation action plan must address any potential resistance.

The first step is to develop a communication method that will inform everyone affected by the change of the objectives of the change. This method should be open, informative, and complete. Individuals must be given reasons to buy into the process modifications. Buy-in by the individuals is necessary to make the application a success.

In addition, the team must decide what actions are necessary to accomplish the stated goals. Who will take the leadership responsibility to ensure that each action is accomplished accurately and in a timely manner? What are people in the new process required to do? What factors will ensure that a change in behavior occurs?

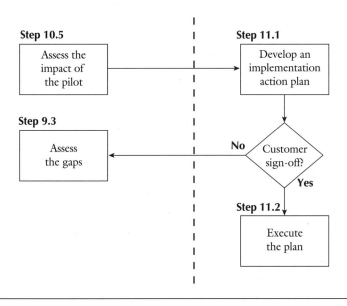

Figure 12.7. Step 11.0. Implement the new process.

The implementation plan should also specify the measurements that will be used to evaluate the new process and how these measurements will be communicated to individuals within the process. Further, these measures should be similar to or a subset of the measures used during the pilot. The measurements should be

- Easily obtainable
- Critical to process performance
- Timely
- Accessible to the individuals who need the feedback

Further, because process changes tend to have a wide impact within the organization, some additional issues need to be addressed in the plan. Specifically, the organization's goals, objectives, and business plans may need revision to incorporate any changes required by the new process. At a microlevel, individual performance objectives may need revision to incorporate changes required by the new process. The plan should also specify how the organization will provide individuals with an upgraded education and skills to ensure the success of the changes, if upgrades are needed. Finally, an appropriate feedback system must be established to provide appropriate and relevant feedback to individuals.

Step 11.2   Execute the plan.

Finally, the organization should execute the implementation action plan and fully implement the reengineered process. However, the RSC must ensure several essentials.

- The stakeholders and the sponsor(s) must lead the implementation, not the reengineering team.
- The customers must buy into the improvements they will receive.

The implementation action plan combined with these small steps will provide a smooth transition between the old and the new processes and will build customer commitment to the change.

Summary

This phase, designing change, provides a method to identify, assess, map, and ultimately, redesign business processes. This section offers a framework for gaining insights into processes and translating those insights into quantum leaps of change.

The reengineering steps presented in this section differ from other process improvement or business process reengineering methods. The difference rests with the two complementary mapping methods—flowcharting and integrated flow diagramming—and the consideration of the culture in which the process operates.

The reason for the two mapping methods is that they provide two different pictures of the process. Flowcharting shows control points and the flow of tasks and activity. It does not, however, map the communication patterns of the process, which tend to differ from the flow of tasks. This mapping of communication patterns occurs in the integrated flow diagram.

Exploring the cultural aspects of the process is important because people make the process work. Old processes may include several cultural aspects that are highly desirable and that should be maintained in the new process. Thus, the reengineering steps presented in this section offers a simple method for analyzing cultural factors of a process.

The reengineering of business processes must be driven by the organization's core competencies and customer requirements. If a process is reengineered without these considerations, a lot of time and energy can be spent changing a process that does not need changing in the first place. In turn, this wasted energy tends to shift to frustration, which can significantly hinder any future reengineering effort.

Appropriately applied, the reengineering steps offered in this section provide a comprehensive approach to the redesign and rebuilding of the organization's business processes. The results gained will significantly outweigh the resources necessary to complete the reengineering effort.

Evaluating Change

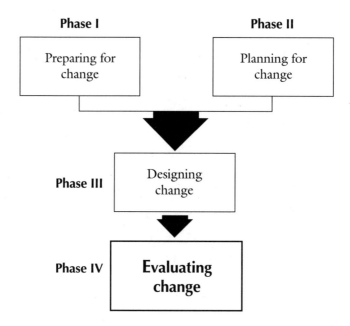

The final phase of the reengineering model is called *evaluating change.* The purpose of this phase is to evaluate the improvement made during the activity of the last year and to develop priorities for the coming year. Specifically, this phase helps determine where the reengineering effort has been and where it should be going in the future.

CHAPTER 13

Evaluating the Improvement

The purpose of this final phase is to evaluate past activity and develop objectives and priorities for the coming year. Feedback from all the reengineering activity along with a review of organizational performance are used in this evaluation. This review parallels the operational review conducted in chapter 7, but this one is more broadly focused.

The evaluation process should be completed at least quarterly so management can verify that the reengineering effort is consistent with operational plans and is on track. If the resulting change has exceeded the anticipated level, then operational plans should be adjusted to prepare for the next year's activities. Next, the organization's strategic plan can also be upgraded and modified on an annual basis to reflect the outcomes of the reengineering effort. These modifications allow the organization to move forward in its continuous efforts to achieve its vision and mission.

The purpose of this chapter, therefore, is to provide an overview of the evaluation process. However, this chapter will not get into the details of metrics and measures; instead, it will highlight the criteria for meaningful measures. It will also briefly explore some of the issues that make designing and applying meaningful measures difficult.

INTRODUCTION

One of reengineering's most important activities is the development of a measurement system that can help set priorities and gauge progress. When an organization quantifies its progress, employees can see the impact they are having and are better able to conform to performance expectations.

A consistent theme in both manufacturing and service organizations is that many departments and individuals feel their jobs do not lend themselves to measurement. This is not true. If a job cannot be measured, then it is probably not a job worth doing and should be eliminated. This statement applies to every level including the CEO. The difference in levels is the direct impact a specific individual has on the measure itself. For example, a factory floor worker could be measured on the number of products produced per hour. This individual can directly affect the measures by either speeding up or slowing down the work pace. On the other hand, a senior vice president of sales could be measured on sales revenue. In this situation, however, the individual is not personally responsible for closing sales. Rather, he or she must motivate the sales force to make more sales. Thus, although this individual's activities have only indirect impact on sales, they can still be measured.

The problem here is that most people don't understand the difference between activities and output. For example, at a local financial institution, the organization's management information system (MIS) department was asked to define what it does. The manager of the department talked about filling out forms, loading programs, and inputting data. In reality, what the manager discussed was activity, not results. In this case, what the department did was generate organized consolidated customer reports. After evaluating what it *really* did, the MIS group changed its measurements from the number of forms processed and programs loaded to the number of customers satisfied with the reports they were receiving. At first, the new measurement reports showed startlingly low satisfaction. Only 41.8 percent of the customers were satisfied with the reports they were receiving. After one year, with the department focused on its true goal, the percentage of good reports delivered increased to 69 percent and after five years, satisfaction was up to 98.6 percent.

At many organizations, measurement provides the underlying foundation to their change efforts. For example, Motorola uses the following three measurements for all activities.[1]

1. Total customer satisfaction

2. Total cycle-time reduction

3. Total defects per unit of work

Measurement also provides a foundation for change at General Dynamics (GD), which has had up to 60 measurement parameters and hundreds of improvement projects. At GD and Motorola, and a variety of other companies, senior-level managers are measured on productivity and quality improvement process results. In addition, measurement (and accountability) is pushed as far down the organization as possible.

The development of a measurement system is the key to any reengineering effort. Only with this type of information can a reengineering team and the organization know if any progress has been made. The next section will examine the criteria for setting up a successful and meaningful measurement system to evaluate change.

CRITERIA FOR MEANINGFUL MEASUREMENTS

In developing a measurement system to evaluate change, six foundation criteria must be considered.

1. Validity

2. Completeness

3. Comparability

4. Inclusiveness

5. Timeliness

6. Cost-effectiveness

Validity

One of the most important criteria of a measurement is that it is *valid*, or that it accurately reflects changes in real productivity. According to the *Random House Dictionary of the English Language*, *valid* means "producing the desired results."[2] Frequently, organizations use measures that are not valid, and this results in a distorted and inaccurate indicator of organizational productivity. An example of this common fault of measurements can be viewed at the warehouse operations for a fictional drug store chain.

At the end of each week, each store manager placed a stock refill order with the area distribution center or warehouse. Upon receipt, the warehouse personnel reviewed each order and pulled the desired items from inventory. Each order varied in the number of items ordered. That is, a store might order a single item, such as baby oil, or several inventory items, such as baby oil, cold medication, and cotton swabs. Originally, management designated *orders filled* as the common unit of measurement and the total number of *orders processed* as the output. In this example, however, the measures provided invalid results. After much discussion and consideration, it was determined that *pulls per hour* was a more valid measure than *orders processed per hour* because the number of pulls recognizes the more critical variable, the number of items on any order. For example, an order consisting of 17 pulls requires more time and labor than one with 5 pulls.

Table 13.1 provides a sample of the data analyzed by management when deciding to use pulls versus orders as the base of measurement. In the first quarter, output (defined by orders) per hour was up only 1.6 percent, and cost per order increased 2.3 percent. While this in itself may not represent a dramatic increase, with pulls used as the output measure, productivity actually increased 9.4 percent, and cost rose only 1.3 percent. Using these figures, the financial groups of this company were able to make more accurate predictions, of future costs. They estimated that, if this increase in productivity and marginal increase in cost

	First quarter	Second quarter	
Measurement components	**Quantity**	**Quality**	**% increase or (decrease)**
Orders processed	16,324	16,848	3.2
Pulls processed	26,882	31,009	15.4
Total worker hours	8,699	8,869	2
Compensation paid	36,971	37,693	2
Analysis			
Compensation per worker hour	4.25	4.25	0
Output per paid hour: Number of orders	1.87	1.9	1.6
Cost per order	.44	.45	2.3
Output per paid hour: Number of pulls	3.2	3.5	9.4
Cost per pull	.73	.82	1.3

Figure 13.1. Sample measurement data, pulls versus orders.

continued over a three-year period, the organization would save about $185,000 in labor costs.

Completeness

To be good, productivity measures must be complete. *Completeness* refers to the thoroughness with which all results delivered and all resources consumed are measured. For example, quarterly production reports provide details on department production levels, profit and loss, and operating costs, which might be sufficient for a plant manager to assess his or her job. On the other hand, this level of completeness most likely would not be sufficient for the first-line supervisor, who needs details at the individual worker level. Thus, completeness is defined according to the needs of the individual who uses the information.

Comparability

The usefulness of measures lies in the ability of users to compare one period to another, or to a specific standard. With comparable measures, an organization is able to determine if it is utilizing available resources more or less efficiently.

Inclusiveness

Measurements should cover a wide range of activities within all functions of the organization. However, in most businesses, manufacturing and service alike, measurements focus on production activities, and then only on a limited number of elements within this production arena, such as the usual labor and materials components. In contrast, they should also include nonproduction components such as cost of quality, sales, equipment, customer services, and facility. Further, an organization should measure the administrative aspects of its company, such as accounting, data processing, and maintenance.

Timeliness

Today, many managers are given production or profit-and-loss reports so far after an activity has occurred that they are unable to respond properly to any problems that may be identified. Whereas continuous or real-time measurements may not be practical, a measurement system should recognize and communicate significant exceptions or deviations from the plan on at least a daily basis to those managers directly responsible.

Cost-effectiveness

The goal behind a measurement system is to assist an organization's leadership to improve organizational results. It does so by increasing managerial awareness, and thus, improves control. Therefore, a key component of a measurement process is that it must be made with regard for the related costs, both direct and indirect.

Managers, not uncommonly, view the measurement process as too time-consuming. Often, they blame a supervisor for forcing them to waste time on measuring that should be devoted to getting the work itself done. And there is some element of truth to such statements. However, the question to answer is this: Does the benefit of focusing solely on getting the work itself done outweigh the costs of lack of awareness and diminishing managerial control—conditions that can result in organizations that forgo measurement? Still, since measuring does not produce revenue, managers must ensure that they use measurement consistently and in proportion to the value of the data derived.

THE DIFFICULTY IN DESIGNING AND IMPLEMENTING MEANINGFUL MEASURES

A number of factors make it difficult to design, apply, and benefit from meaningful measures. In fact, many organizations have developed measurement systems only later to discard the results or scrap the entire system. Thus, developing a meaningful measurement system is easier said than done. Let's briefly explore why.

If an organization produces the same product or provides the same service year after year, measurement is relatively simple. Even with an organization that produces a number of products or provides a variety of services, the different outputs can be added and the sum used as the measure of outputs. However, the outputs can be added and the sum used as the measure of outputs only if the products and services remain unchanged and are used in exactly the same mix or proportions from period to period. The problem is that this is seldom the case. Products and services tend to be modified as time passes. New offerings are introduced as old ones are dropped. The product mix changes.

Generally, five primary difficulties arise when an organization is establishing a measurement system.

1. The measurements tend to be too broad.

2. The measurements tend to be activity oriented rather than results oriented.

3. Management does not provide enough resources to do to job.

4. The system fails to define responsibilities.

5. The measurement system's integrity is compromised.

Measurement broadness

If a front line supervisor responsible for daily results receives only quarterly production or profit and loss statements, this would be of little benefit. Sometimes measurements implemented by an organization tend to be so broad that they only communicate that *something* is wrong, with no clue as to where the problem might lie. Thus, it is important not only that enough measurements be applied and at the right places but also that each level of management has the benefits of those measures best suited to its needs. Frontline supervisors have a real need for the daily detail information. On the other hand, executives tend to require fewer and more broadly based measures for their evaluation needs.

Activity versus results orientation

Sometimes within an organization, managerial focus drifts to the hustle and bustle of activity with diminished regard for results. The trap of conducting and measuring activity for the sake of the activity rather than focusing on the results occurs commonly. This problem can be avoided if the organization focuses on the work process in terms of the results it is trying to achieve rather than on the activity it conducts.

Resources

In all professional sporting events, several individuals occupy the playing floor in addition to the athletes themselves. Basketball has two additional persons on the floor, and hockey and football have three, composing what is called the chain-gang—individuals that do nothing but measure the progress in advancing the ball. Can you imagine a professional sporting event that did not measure progress and results? Yet in the game of big business, where the stakes are very high, people often resist adding measurement resources to gauge the organization's progress toward its goals. For an organization to be successful, it must measure its results, and in most cases, this requires additional resources.

Responsibility

All individuals within an organization must be held accountable for the organization's performance. In many organizations, useful measurement systems are set up, but no one is specifically responsible for the results. In this situation, when a problem arises, everyone points a finger at everyone else. This finger pointing and buck passing will be minimized when responsibility is unequivocally fixed. The measurement system and supporting accountability should be extended as far down the organization as possible to produce the best results. That is, the individual who does the work should measure and be held accountable for the results, either positive or negative.

On the other hand, some organizations overemphasize accountability at the expense of motivation. In these cases, managers have substituted threats, real or implied, for encouragement and other intangible rewards. Managers whose thinking is overly dominated by such a punitive ethic will very likely destroy the motivation of their employees in the process of making certain that "no one gets away with anything." Therefore, an organization needs to find a balance between too much and too little accountability. The manager who bases accountability on the assumption that people will work properly if their internal system of values and sense of fairness are not violated can maintain a constructive and productive work environment.

Integrity

The integrity of a measurement system can be compromised for many reasons. One example can be found in manufacturing. At a molded plastics company in the Southwest, a series of quality control measures were established for all workers to follow. If the numbers, or acceptable product going out the door, were too low as the end of the month approached, supervisors pushed product out the door. They did not care whether this product met quality control standards, since they were evaluated on volume, not on volume that conformed to customer standards.

Besides pressure for numbers, or results, other factors in the work environment can increase the probability that measurements will be compromised. First, the measurement documents may be so cumbersome or complicated that they encourage the persons assigned the measurement responsibility to take error-inducing shortcuts. Further, a system that measures only output may provide no credit for coping with uncontrollable problems, such as defective material provided by a supplier.

However, many methods exist for developing and applying compromise-resistant measurements. These include systems that have realistic goals and that use measurements to elicit good performance from employees.

FINAL REENGINEERING STEPS

This final reengineering phase has only two remaining steps.

Step 12.0 Review and evaluate progress.
  Step 12.1 Evaluate organizational measures.
  Step 12.2 Have the steering committee evaluate the results.
  Step 12.3 Revise the three- to five-year strategic plan, if necessary.
Step 13.0 Repeat yearly operational/breakthrough planning cycle (Step 5.0).

The rationale behind these final steps should be clear from the preceding discussions.

Notes

1. Motorola's "Quality Briefing" provides detailed information regarding these three measures. To obtain information about this event, contact Motorola in Schaumburg, Illinois, at 800-446-6744.

2. *Random House Dictionary of the English Language.* (New York: Random House, 1969), 1076.

PHASE IV

Summary

The need to measure and thereby improve productivity of an organization is paramount. For an organization to improve and increase productivity and, ultimately, market share and profitability, it needs valid and complete measurements applied to a broad range of activities and processes.

Several obstacles hinder the application of meaningful measurements, including management's reluctance to provide the required measurement resources. Meaningful measurements require resources and an unwavering management commitment. They also maximize the organization's core competencies and realize the organization's potential through increased employee awareness and accountability.

Concluding
Comments

The business environment is in a constant state of change. The economic shift that is occurring is producing a new economy and the advent of this new economy—however postindustrial—does not mean the end of industry, just as the Industrial Revolution did not mean the end of agriculture. The true shift of this or any economy occurs when we adopt a new, all-encompassing model. The shift that must occur now is to stop using mechanistic, industrial models to run today's complex industrial-service economy.

Albert Einstein said that new frameworks or models are like climbing a mountain; the larger view encompasses rather than rejects the earlier, more restrictive view. Today, for example, the industrial sector consists of manufacturers such as car companies that are also credit institutions, and major consumer product manufacturers that finance purchases and issue credit cards. The financial sector is being blurred and changed as never before.[1]

One hallmark of the ambiguous new economy is the need to define businesses in terms of customers' changing needs and what the company does best. Many service giants in the industrial period learned this lesson, and for this reason, they are now undergoing the most massive transformations in their histories. For example, Aetna Life and Casualty, one of the most successful models of service organizations and, with $90 billion in assets, the nation's largest publicly traded insurance company, is completely revamping its business because of this new economy reality.

Aetna's underchairman and CEO Ronald E. Compton is reengineering vital functions in all of Aetna's business units. The company is focusing on the customer as a prized asset. Over the years, business processes evolved that were in the best interest of the company and were followed with religious devotion. To achieve its refocus, Aetna eliminated business processes that were not customer focused and is replacing them with technology-driven concepts and methods.

According to Compton, seven commandments are inherent to a reengineering effort.[2]

1. Give people a mission, a clear understanding of how to achieve that mission, and a road map for choosing the appropriate steps for action.

2. Either serve customers superbly or don't even try.

3. Change is not something that happens by itself. It's a way of life. It's not a process; it's a value. It's not something you do; it engulfs you.

4. Technology is never really the problem. The problem is how to use technology effectively.

5. The wrong answer rarely kills you. What it does is waste time. Further, time is a limited resource—the only absolutely limited one.

6. The weak link in reengineering is will. Reengineering is a huge job, and it is agonizingly, heartbreakingly tough.

7. Once people catch on to reengineering, you can't hold them down. It's a lifetime venture.

Thus, reengineering an organization calls for near-heroic belief, dedication, and effort. It requires resources, both time and money.

Finally, a successful reengineering effort affects every person and every part of your business. Thus, a reengineered corporation must and will be transformed at all levels.

Is it worth the effort necessary to reengineer an organization? Ask Compton. He states that Aetna is expecting to save more than $120 million annually from streamlining its work processes. Or you can ask any salesperson who represents a company with products or services that have a tainted reputation.

Companies that are constantly changing to meet the needs of their customers and anticipating new customer requirements or new markets do not accomplish these tasks by sheer luck. These companies prepare and plan their actions in advance. They put into action the steps of organizational reengineering by preparing for change, by planning for change, by designing the change, and by evaluating the change. They overwhelm their competitors by directing their efforts and resources in smarter ways. They focus on their organization's core competencies. They spoil their customers not from altruism but purely out of self-interest. Their focus is on the customer at all times. They determine what the customer expects, and they exceed those expectations.

To succeed, a company must be a leader rather than a follower. Companies that are content to be followers teeter on the edge of a cliff. A few nudges from the leaders, a few years of rising customer expectations, and followers tend to topple. Once over the edge, followers start a cycle downward. Dissatisfied customers vent their rage and frustration on employees, who react by providing shoddier service—which only makes customers more dissatisfied. Followers in this downward cycle must ask not whether or when to start a reengineering effort, but rather, how to start and follow through with one.

In sum, the only course for organizations interested in survival is to forge ahead and reengineer the way they do business. However, putting the elements of reengineering into practice is not simple. Just ask the management at organizations as diverse as Cadillac, Beacon Hotels, Motorola, Federal Express, Aetna, Amoco, and Hallmark.

There are a few cautions as you decide to tackle reengineering: many are based on Compton's seven commandments. Review those seven commandments and learn from them. Further, do not be discouraged if you make mistakes. Mistakes waste only time—if we learn from them. The most common mistake is exemplified with the following story.

A man was looking on the ground for his lost keys. When his neighbor asked him where he lost them, he pointed to a different place. 'Then, why aren't you looking over there?' asked the neighbor. The man replied, 'because the light is better over here.'

Much like this man, we waste time if we change one part of an organization simply because that part is easier to change or can be changed with fewer political problems. That is not to say that less critical parts should not be reengineered. However, if we waste time, money, and profit on reengineering less problematic areas of our organization, we miss the major breakthroughs that can come from reengineering critical processes—that is, we miss the benefits of reengineering.

The benefits of reengineering an organization far outweigh the cost, for the cost of not changing can be the very existence of an organization. The business environment of today requires that all companies change—change to meet customer expectations and change to remain profitable. Organizational reengineering is designed to facilitate that change.

Notes

1. General Motors and General Electric are now in the credit card business and can raise money more cheaply and more easily by issuing their own commerical loans than by using a bank's services. The Big Three (Ford, Chrysler, and General Motors) finance car loans for customers directly and often make more money on financing a

car than on manufacturing it. Finally, the line between commercial and investment banks in the new economy has blurred. Specifically, as the Glass-Stewagall Act becomes unraveled, the jobs of commercial, corporate finance experts, and capital market traders become interrelated.

2. Rifkin, Glenn. "Reengineering Aetna." *Forbes ASAP*, A Technology Supplement to *Forbes* Magazine. Sidebar (June 7, 1993): 81.

Additional Readings

ORGANIZATIONAL CHANGE

Albrecht, K. *The Creative Corporation*. Homewood, Ill.: Dow Jones-Irwin, 1987.

Byrne, B. *Habits of Wealth: 111 Proven Entrepreneurial Strategies for Achieving and Leading in the '90s*. Sioux Falls, S.Dak.: Performance One Publications, 1992.

Gardfield, C. A. *Second to None: How Our Smartest Companies Put People First*. Homewood, Ill.: Business One Irwin, 1992.

Kanter, R. M. *The Change Masters: Innovations for Productivity in the American Corporation*. New York: Simon and Schuster, 1983.

Keidel, R. W. *Corporate Players: Designs for Working and Winning Together*. New York: John Wiley and Sons, 1988.

Martel, L. *Mastering Change: The Key to Business Success*. New York: Simon and Schuster, 1986.

Naisbitt, J., and P. Aburdene. *Re-inventing the Corporation: Transforming Your Job and Your Company for the New Informational Society.* New York: Warner Books, 1985.

Stewart J., Jr. *Managing a Successful Business Turnaround.* New York: AMACOM, 1984.

Waterman, R. H. *The Renewal Factor: How the Best Get and Keep the Competitive Edge.* Toronto and New York: Bantam Books, 1987.

PLANNING

Cooper, G. A. *The Business Plan Workbook.* Englewood Cliffs, N.J.: Prentice Hall, 1989.

Gumpert, D. E. *Inc. Magazine* Presents How to Really Create a Success Business Plan: Featuring the Business Plans for Pizza Hut, People Express, Ben & Jerry's Ice Cream, Celestial Seasoning. Boston: Inc. Publications, 1990.

Hanan, M. *Tomorrow's Competition: The Next Generation of Growth Strategies.* New York: AMACOM, 1991.

McLaughlin, H. J. *The Entrepreneur's Guide to Building a Better Business Plan: A Step-by-Step Approach.* New York: John Wiley and Sons, 1992.

Olins, W. *Corporate Identity: Making Business Strategy Visible Through Design.* Boston: Harvard Business School Press, 1989.

Primozic, K. and J. Leben. *Strategic Choices: Supremacy, Survival, or Sayonara.* New York: McGraw-Hill, 1991.

Steiner, G. A. *Strategic Planning: What Every Manager Must Know.* New York: Free Press, 1979.

Touchie, R. *Preparing a Successful Business Plan: A Practical Guide for Small Business.* North Vancouver, B.C., and Bellingham, Wash.: International Self-Counsel Press, 1989.

PROCESS MANAGEMENT

Boedecker, R. F. *Eleven Conditions for Excellence: The IBM Total Quality Improvement Process.* Boston: American Institute of Management, 1989.

Brassard, M. *The Memory Jogger Plus +.* Methuen, Mass.: Goal/QPC, 1989.

Harshbarger, R. *Process Analysis Technique.* Chicago: Macmillan-McGraw Hill, 1988.

Kane, E. J. "IBM's Quality Focus on the Business Process." *Quality Progress* 20 (April 1986): 24.

King, R. "Listening to the Voice of the Customer: Using Quality Function Deployment Systems." *National Productivity Review* 6 (Summer 1987): 27.

McCabe, W. J. "Quality Methods Applied to the Business Process." Paper presented at ASQC's 40th Annual Quality Congress, 1986.

Melan, E. H. "Focus on the Process: Key to Quality Improvement." Paper presented at ASQC's 42nd Annual Quality Congress, 1988.

———. *Process Management: Methods for Improving Products and Services.* Milwaukee, Wisc.: ASQC Quality Press; New York: McGraw-Hill, 1993.

————. "Process Management: A Unifying Framework for Improvement." *National Productivity Review* 8, no. 4 (Autumn 1989): 61.

Nadler, G. *Work Design.* Homewood, Ill.: Richard Irwin, 1970.

Shaw, G. T. "Process Quality Focus." Paper presented at the ASQC Business Process Improvement Symposium, Washington D.C., March 21, 1988.

Shostack, G. L. "Designing Services that Deliver." *Harvard Business Review* 62 (Jan./Feb. 1984): 118.

Zachman, J. W. "Developing and Executing Business Strategies Using Process Quality Management." Paper presented at IMPRO90, Juran Institute, Wilton, Conn., 1989.

Index